Napoléon

Bernard Chevallier
Conservateur en chef du Musée National du Château de Malmaison

With Introduction by
Jean Tulard
President of the Institut Napoléon

Historical Essay by
Christophe Pincemaille

Translation by
Thomas Michael Gunther

Presented by
WONDERS
The Memphis International Cultural Series
a division of the City of Memphis, Tennessee
in association with
The French Museum System
and other major collections

This exhibition is supported by an indemnity from the
Federal Council on the Arts and the Humanities.

Library of Congress Cataloging-in-Publication Data

Chevallier, Bernard, 1936-
   Napoleon / Bernard Chevallier ; with introduction by Jean Tulard ;
historical essay by Christophe Pincemaille ; translation by Thomas
Michael Gunther.
      p.   cm.
   ISBN 1-882516-02-8 (hard cover) : $49.95. — ISBN 1-882516-03-6
(soft cover) : $19.95
   1. Napoleon I, Emperor of the French, 1769-1821. 2. France—Kings
and rulers—Biography.   3. History in art—Pictorial works.
   4. Napoleon I, Emperor of the French, 1769-1821—Art patronage-
-Catalogs.   I. Pincemaille, Christophe.   II. Title.
DC203.8C54   1993
944.05'092—dc20
   [B]   93-10210
                                                                         CIP

Published by Lithograph Publishing Company,
a division of Lithograph Printing Company

Project Manager: Russ Gordon
Editor: Liz Conway
Contributing Editors: Dory Davis Smith, Geoffrey Smith
Technical Editors: Elizabeth Richter Bowers, Sherred Hudson
Graphic Design/Production Coordination: Sheila Hudson
Assistant Designer: Janet Dicken
Typography and Composition: Debra Langford Cupps, The Composing Room, Inc.
Color Separations and Printing: Lithograph Printing Company

Photography of Exhibition Items (credits are referenced by catalogue numbers): Atelier de
Breuil-Lautard: 4, 5, 17; Berger, Nyon: 162, 163; Bibliothèque Nationale, Paris: 42; Raoul
Brunon: 180-186; Jean-Loup Charmet: 59, 161; Cliché photothèque des musées de la Ville
de Paris © SPADEM: 60, 120, 154, 157, 158, 179; J.-P. Elie: 139, 208; Fondation Napoléon:
165-168, 177; L. Sully Jaulmes: 77, 80, 82, 85; Hubert Josse: 2, 3, 6-8, 10, 11, 13, 16, 27,
28, 32, 38, 41, 43, 55, 70, 81, 83, 92-95, 99, 102, 107-109, 140, 143, 145, 153, 155, 159,
160, 164, 175, 187, 189, 190, 197, 206, 207, 209, 210, 214; Konrad Keller: 211; Pascal
Lemaitre: 119, 200; Mobilier National, Paris: 84, 86, 88-91, 96, 170-172, 174; Monuments
historiques, Musée National du Château de Malmaison: 54; Musée de l'Armée, Paris: 30, 31,
39, 40, 64, 178, 188, 205; Musée d'Art et d'Histoire, Palais Masséna, Nice: 144; Musée des
Beaux-Arts, Nantes: 33; Musée Chaumet, Paris: 67, 69, 137, 148, 150, 152; Musée
Marmottan -Claude Monet, Paris: 9, 12, 14; Musée National du Château de Malmaison:
141; Musée National de la Légion d'Honneur et des Ordres de Chevalerie, Paris: 176;
Museum of Fine Arts, Boston, S. A. Denio Collection: cat. no. 23; National Archives,
Washington, D.C.: 58; National Museum of Natural History, Smithsonian Institution,
Washington, D.C.: 149, 151; Photo Vatican Museums: 68; Roger Prigent: 1; Réunion des
Musées Nationaux: 15, 19-22, 24-26, 29, 34-37, 44-53, 56, 57, 61-63, 65, 66, 71-76, 78,
79, 87, 97, 98, 100, 101, 103-106, 110-118, 121-136, 138, 146, 147, 156, 169, 173, 191-196,
198, 199, 201, 212, 213, 215; Larry Stein: 18; Van Cleef & Arpels, New York: 142;
Wellington Museum, Apsley House, London: 202-204.

Collateral Photography: Proctor Jones Collection: p. 26, p. 38; Tallandier (de Jardine); Jack
Kyle: p. 35, 40; Louvre: p. 31, 33, © Photo R.M.N.; © National Geographic Society: p. 23,
Joseph J. Scherschel; p. 41, 176 Gordon W. Gahan; p. 42, Quentin Keynes; Versailles: p. 34.

Cartography: Thomas Nathan: p. 37, 42.

CONTENTS

A Message from the Mayor of the City of Memphis   4

A Message from the Ambassador of France   5

A Message from the Honorary Committee Chairman   6

French Committee   7

WONDERS: The Memphis International Cultural Series   8

Lenders to the Exhibition   11

Sponsors   12

Contributors   13

A Statement from the Curator of the Exhibition
Bernard Chevallier   14

Introduction
Jean Tulard   15

Genealogy of the Bonaparte Family   17

Chronology of Napoleon Bonaparte's Career   18

Napoleon   21
    Background and Napoleon's Youth, 1769-1793   23
    The Young General Proves Himself, 1793-1799   26
    The First Consul, 1800-1804   30
    Napoleon Emperor, 1804   32
    The Emperor at War, 1805-1814   36
    Elba and Saint Helena, 1814-1821   40

Catalogue of the Exhibition   45

A Message from the
MAYOR OF THE CITY OF MEMPHIS

Few figures in history have inscribed their name as indelibly in the annals of mankind as Napoleon Bonaparte.

With the 1993 presentation of the exhibition *Napoleon*, organized by WONDERS: The Memphis International Cultural Series and the French National Museum System, the already legendary status of the Emperor Napoleon I will be significantly augmented.

Through the *Napoleon* exhibition, further enlightenment into the rich mosaic of world history continues to be manifested in the lives of hundreds of thousands of citizens from Memphis, the mid-America region, the Nation, and the world over.

Malmaison, the Louvre, Fontainebleau, Versailles, and other museums and private collections in France, Switzerland, Italy, the Vatican, England, and the United States have generously provided this rare opportunity to experience first-hand the artistic and historical treasures of Napoleon.

Since the beginning of our country's history, France has associated itself with the United States in the cause of freedom and democracy. Now some two hundred years later, this most valued relationship continues and flourishes.

On behalf of the citizens of Memphis, I wish to express my profound gratitude to His Imperial Highness Prince Napoleon for serving as the Honorary Chairman of the exhibition and to President François Mitterrand, Minister of National Education and of Culture Jack Lang, Minister of Defense Pierre Joxe, Ambassador Jacques Andréani, Consul General Jacky Musnier, Director of the Museums of France Jacques Sallois, and Chief Conservator of the National Museum of the Château of Malmaison and Curator of the *Napoleon* exhibition Bernard Chevallier, all of whom have played a significant role in the development of this historic cultural achievement.

Finally, I wish to call special attention to the vital role of WONDERS: The Memphis International Cultural Series in establishing Memphis as an important cultural center. The legacy of past and the anticipation of future exhibitions and other events organized by this outstanding organization of the City of Memphis promises a bright future for our city.

Dr. W. W. Herenton
Mayor
City of Memphis

A Message from the
AMBASSADOR OF FRANCE

The French Republican Army, commanded by General Bonaparte, entered Memphis in 1797. Not Memphis, Tennessee, but rather Memphis, Egypt... For that matter, the State of Tennessee was but one year old in 1797. Yet the history of Memphis, Tennessee, was marked nevertheless by that of France: France's Louisiana Territory extended far beyond what is now the State of Louisiana, and was bordered on the east by the Mississippi River. It was this vast territory that the First Consul of the French Republic ceded to the United States of America by virtue of the Treaty of 10 Floreal Year XI of the Republic (April 30, 1803, by American reckoning)—and that First Consul was none other than Napoleon Bonaparte.

We owe the image of General Bonaparte crossing the Alps in the footsteps of Hannibal and Charlemagne—a scene dramatized by the canvas reproduced in this catalogue to Jacques-Louis David, a great artist whose tumultuous life mirrored the history of his time. Already famous under the monarchy, the quasi-official artist of the Revolution and the Empire died in exile after a coalition of European monarchies finally defeated France in 1815.

David could have sought refuge in the United States, as did Joseph Lakanal, the founder of France's public education system, and so many other revolutionaries and companions of Emperor Napoleon, who were warmly welcomed after Waterloo. Thus, the fact that many national and private French collections have sent exceptional pieces from this equally exceptional historical period is apt indeed—a sort of expression of gratitude to be underscored by the participation of France's elite *Garde Républicaine* at the exhibition's inaugural ceremonies on April 22, 1993.

Napoleon in Memphis will be one of this year's major events highlighting French culture in the United States. I hope that all those who helped bring about this exhibition, organized by WONDERS: The Memphis International Cultural Series, find in it France's expression of friendship and gratitude.

Jacques Andréani
Ambassador of France
to the United States of America

By organizing this magnificent exhibition, the City of Memphis commemorates in the United States the prestigious accomplishments of the Emperor Napoleon the First, my great-granduncle.

There are numerous ties between my family and the United States of America:

Historic ties—I have only to mention the treaty of 1803 by which the Louisiana Territory became part of the United States, during the Consulate of Napoleon Bonaparte.

Family ties as well—young Jerome Bonaparte, my great-grandfather, the Emperor's younger brother, chose a young Baltimore patrician, Elizabeth Patterson, as his first wife, and their descendants lived in the United States until the 1930s. After 1815, King Joseph, another brother of the Emperor, took up residence for many years at Point Breeze in Delaware.

Today, I am happy to see this splendid retrospective create new ties and render homage to Franco-American friendship.

His Imperial Highness
Prince Napoleon

FRENCH COMMITTEE

UNDER THE PATRONAGE OF

His Excellency François Mitterrand
President of the Republic of France

HONORARY COMMITTEE

His Imperial Highness Prince Napoleon
Honorary Committee Chairman

His Excellency Jack Lang
Minister of National Education and of Culture

His Excellency Pierre Joxe
Minister of Defense

His Excellency Jacques Andréani
Ambassador of France to the United States of America

The Honorable Jacques Chirac
Mayor of Paris

Jacques Sallois
Director of the Museums of France

The Honorable Jacky Musnier
Consul General of the Republic of France

Pierre Lemoine
Honorary Inspector General of Museums

Annie Cohen-Solal
Cultural Counselor
French Cultural Services

Jean Mendelson
Counselor of Press and Information Service
of the French Embassy

Jacques Solillou
Cultural Attaché
French Cultural Services

Pierre Bayle
Technical Counselor of the Ministry of Defense

The Baron Gourgaud
President of the Fondation Napoléon

Charles-Otto Zieseniss
Vice-President of the Fondation Napoléon

EXHIBITION CURATOR

Bernard Chevallier
Chief Conservator of the National Museum
of the Château of Malmaison

WONDERS

THE MEMPHIS INTERNATIONAL CULTURAL SERIES

EXECUTIVE STAFF

Jon K. Thompson, *Executive Director*
Dollie Hardy, *Executive Secretary*

SPECIAL PROJECTS

Sheryl O. Bowen, *Manager*
Salpy Boyadjian, *Gift Shop Manager*
Bill Wedgeworth, *Volunteer/Operations Coordinator*
Vernetta Anderson, *Volunteer Assistant Coordinator*
Eldra Tarpley, *Special Events/Operations Coordinator*

LOGISTICS AND ADMINISTRATION

Glen A. Campbell, *Manager*
Marie Kirk Owens, *Coordinator of Finance*
Janet Brown, *Administrative Assistant*
E. Warren Perry, *Logistics Assistant*
Barbara Gales, *Receptionist*

DESIGN AND CONSTRUCTION

John Conroy, *Manager*
Ron Griffin, *Assistant Manager*

MARKETING

Twyla Dixon, *Manager*
Helen Bailey, *Secretary*
Jack Kyle, *Public Relations and Communications Manager*
Jodi Ball, *Group Sales and Special Events Coordinator*
Tracey Ballard, *Ticketing and Sales Coordinator*
Tony Harley, *Ticketing and Sales Assistant Coordinator*

SECURITY

Commander Michael Lee, Sr., *Manager*
Lieutenant David Booker, *Assistant Manager*

CURATORIAL AND EDUCATIONAL SERVICES

Steve Masler, *Manager*
Susan Danciger, *Curatorial Assistant*

COMMUNITY AND CORPORATE DEVELOPMENT

Narquenta Sims, *Manager*

SPECIAL PROJECTS
Sheryl O. Bowen, *Manager*

GIFT SHOP
Salpy Boyadjian, *Manager*
Velma Johnson, *Assistant Manager*
Nancy Robinson, *Assistant Manager*
The Bancroft Group, *Consultant*
Advance Manufacturing Company,
  Display Cases

VOLUNTEER ADMINISTRATION
Bill Wedgeworth, *Coordinator*
Vernetta Anderson, *Assistant Coordinator*
Emily Bisso, *Day Manager*
K. Sage Lambert, *Day Manager*
Barbara Lee, *Day Manager*

RECORDED TOUR
Dean Daniels, *Operations Manager*
Sean Downes, *Operations Manager*
Robert Niederhauser, *Operations Manager*
Beverly Oliver, *Operations Manager*
Patrick Steinberg, *Operations Manager*
Michelle Tribble, *Operations Manager*
Antenna Theatre
  Chris Tellis, *Director*
  Gregory Peck, *Narrator*

RESTAURANT
Public Eye Catering Company
  David Sorin and Martin Winston, *Owners*
  Phyllis Winston, *Manager*
  Rosie Wills, *Director of Group Sales*

SPECIAL EVENTS
Eldra Tarpley, *Coordinator*
Judy Boshwit, *Calligrapher*

EXHIBITION OPERATIONS
Bill Wedgeworth, *Coordinator*
Eldra Tarpley, *Coordinator*

GALA PRODUCTION
Grand Gatherings
  Jo Bridges
  Cordell Ingram

LOGISTICS AND ADMINISTRATION
Glen A. Campbell, *Manager*
Janet Brown, *Administrative Assistant*
E. Warren Perry, *Logistics Assistant*
Barbara Gales, *Receptionist*

FINANCE
Marie K. Owens, *Coordinator*
Helen Richardson, *Assistant Coordinator*

CATALOGUE PRODUCTION
Bernard Chevallier, *Author*
Christophe Pincemaille, *Historical Text*
Thomas Michael Gunther,
  Translator and Catalogue Assistant
Lithograph Publishing Company
Division of Lithograph Printing Company
  Russ Gordon, *Project Manager*
  Liz Conway, *Editor*
  Sheila Hudson, *Graphic Designer/
    Production Coordinator*
  Janet Dicken, *Assistant Designer*
  Debra Langford Cupps, *Typographer*
  Hubert Josse, *Photographer*

INSURANCE
Allen Insurance Associates
  Robert F. Salmon
  Frederick Schmid
Treadwell & Harry
  Timmons L. Treadwell, III
  Milton LaGasse
  George Urban
Gras Savoye

OBJECT HANDLING AND INSTALLATION
André Chenue & Fils Internationaux
  Pierre Chenue
  Jacques Gaudin
  Isabelle Briand

CUSTOMS HANDLING
Alexander International

MEMPHIS COOK CONVENTION CENTER
Jim Rout, *Chairman of the Board*
Doug Tober, *General Manager*
Nancy Keathley, *Executive Assistant*

DOMESTIC AND INTERNATIONAL TRAVEL
Janet Brown, *Coordinator*
Delta Air Lines, Inc.
  Nikkie G. Taylor,
    District Marketing Supervisor
  Debbie Carney
  Milly Daniel
  Knoverlean Gaston
  Rosemary Rodgers
  Carol Smith
  Ruth Wood
The Peabody Hotel
Holiday Inn Crowne Plaza

MARKETING
Twyla Dixon, *Manager*
Helen Bailey, *Secretary*

GROUP SALES AND SPECIAL EVENTS
Jodi Ball, *Coordinator*
LaMonté Westbrook, *Mail Supervisor*

TICKETING AND SALES
Tracey Ballard, *Coordinator*
Tony Harley, *Assistant Coordinator*
Karen Carter, *Supervisor*
Erin Krastins, *Supervisor*

ADVERTISING AND MARKETING SERVICES
Sossaman Bateman McCuddy Advertising, Inc.
  Ken Sossaman, *President*
  Donna Gordy, *Vice President*
  Elise Mitchell, *Vice President,
    Public Relations*
  Rikki Boyce, *Co-Creative Director*
  Eric Melkent, *Co-Creative Director*
  Beth Graber, *Director, Media Services*

VISITOR SERVICES
Memphis Convention & Visitors Bureau
  Kevin Kane, *President*
  Darrell Ledet, *Vice-President,
    Convention Development*
  Regina Bearden, *Director,
    Tourist Development*
  Dorothy Davis, *Director,
    Visitor Information Services*
  Mary Schmitz, *Director, Communications*

TRAVEL SERVICES
Unique Planning Network
  Maudie Kite-Powell, *President*

SALES VIDEO PRODUCTION
WMC-TV
  Ronald Klayman, *Vice President
    and General Manager*
Memphis Restaurant Association
Metropolitan Memphis Hotel & Motel Association
Memphis Convention & Visitors Bureau
The Peabody Hotel

COMMUNICATIONS AND PUBLIC RELATIONS
Jack Kyle, *Manager*

GRAND INAUGURAL CEREMONY
The Batterie-Fanfare of the Garde Republicaine
  Colonel Antoine Lapadu-Hargues, *Chef d'Etat-Major*
The United States Army Herald Trumpets
  Captain Thomas H. Palmatier, *Director*
The United States Marine Drum & Bugle Corps
  Lieutenant Colonel Truman Crawford, *Director*
Tennessee Air National Guard
  General Mike Butler
WMC-TV5
  Ronald Klayman, *Vice-President
    and General Manager*
Carlos Domenech Photography
The Peabody Hotel
Holiday Inn Crowne Plaza
Brownestone Hotel
Memphis Area Transit Authority
Baldridge Studios
Overton High School Band
  Chris Piecuch, *Director*
Delta Air Lines, Inc. Volunteer Team
Malco Theatres

TENNESSEE DEPARTMENT OF TOURIST DEVELOPMENT
The Honorable Sandra Ford Fulton, *Commissioner*

PARIS MEDIA TOUR
Delta Air Lines, Inc.
  Nikki G. Taylor, *District Marketing Supervisor*
  Debbie Carney
  Francis Conner
  Jackie Pate
  Patrice Miles
  Rodolphe J. Nadeau, *Paris*
  Rosemary Rodgers
  Ruth Wood
Le Meridien Paris Etoile Hotel
Embassy of France
  Jean Mendelsohn, *Counselor,*
    Press & Information
  Anne-Marie Daris
  Karen Taylor
U.S. Embassy, Paris
  Mary Eleanor Gawronski, *Cultural Counselor*
  Jerry L. Prillaman, *Director, Press Service*
Reunion des Musées Nationaux, France
  Sylvie Poujade, *Press Relations*

DESIGN AND CONSTRUCTION
John Conroy, *Manager*
Ron Griffin, *Assistant Manager*

EXHIBITION DESIGN
Nathan, Evans, Pounders, & Taylor
  Louis Pounders, *Architect*
  Tom Nathan
  Clayton Gott
  Phillip Perkins
  Clare Stallings
  Tom Wade

DESIGN AND INSTALLATION CONSULTANT
Quenroe Associates, Inc.
  Elroy Quenroe
  Charles Mack
  David Hamill
  Allyson Smith

ENGINEERING CONSULTANT
Ellers, Oakley, Chester & Rike, Inc.

EXHIBITION CONSTRUCTION
Jameson-Vaccaro Construction Company
  Gene Gibson, *President*
  Chris Jameson, *Secretary-Treasurer*
  William "Butch" Jenné, Jr., *Superintendent*
Advance Manufacturing Company
  David Craig, *President*

10

CURATORIAL AND EDUCATIONAL SERVICES
Steve Masler, *Manager*
Thomas Michael Gunther,
  Curatorial Consultant
Susan Danciger, *Curatorial Assistant*
Jean Lamar, *Staff Assistant*

ARTS FOR THE BLIND AND VISUALLY IMPAIRED
Dr. John Hughes, *President*

EXHIBIT LABEL EDITOR
Barbara Moses

TEACHERS GUIDE
Amelia Barton, *Coordinator*
Arts In Schools Institute
Memphis Arts Council
  Jeff Kratschmer, *Art Direction,*
    Layout and Design
  Kenneth Laird, *Cover Illustration*
  Rebecca Argall, *Writer*
  Tamah Halfacre, *Writer*
  Lee McMahon, *Writer*
  Judith Thompson, *Writer*

DOCENT TRAINING
Maryanne Hickey MacDonald, *Director of*
  Short Courses, Memphis State University
Mary Scheuner, *Director of Education,*
  Memphis Brooks Museum of Art
Leslie Luebbers, *Director,*
  Memphis State University Gallery
Laura Richens, *Lecturer*
Carla Albertson, *Lecturer*
Marilyn Masler, *Curatorial Associate,*
  Memphis Brooks Museum of Art

SPEAKERS BUREAU
Marjorie Gerald, *Coordinator*

PHOTOGRAPHIC SERVICES
Vance Commercial Color Lab
  Percy Campbell

INTRODUCTORY VIDEO
National Geographic Society
  Todd A. Gipstein, *Director*
    of Multi-Image Production

FEDERAL INDEMNIFICATION
National Endowment for the Arts
  Alice M. Whelihan,
    Indemnity Administrator
Butterfield and Butterfield Fine Arts Appraisers
  Alan Fausel, *Director European Paintings*
Malmaison Antiques
  Roger Prigent, *President*

SECURITY
Commander Michael Lee, Sr., *Manager*
Lieutenant David Booker, *Assistant Manager*
Frank Tarrance, *Communications*
Tim Morrow, *Communications*

ELECTRONIC SECURITY
Lectrolarm Custom Systems, Inc.
  William V. Smith, *President*

COMMUNITY AND CORPORATE DEVELOPMENT
Narquenta Sims, *Manager*
The Bancroft Group, *Consultant*

CITY OF MEMPHIS
MEMPHIS POLICE DEPARTMENT
Melvin T. Burgess, *Director*
Eddie B. Adair, *Deputy Director*
Joe M. Holt, *Inspector*

DIVISION OF FINANCE AND ADMINISTRATION
Rick Masson, *Director*
Danny Wray, *Comptroller*
David Crum, *Deputy Comptroller*
Charles Lucas, *Purchasing Agent*
Don Morris, *Manager, Accounts Payable*

DIVISION OF GENERAL SERVICES
Lewis S. Fort, *Director*
Darrell Eldred, *Technical Services*
Brenda Vick, *Printing Supervisor*
Richard Aitken, *Manager of Property Maintenance*
John Stewart, *General Manager*

DIVISION OF PUBLIC WORKS
Benny Lendermon, *Director*
Rodney "Butch" Eder, *Assistant Director*
Frank Pike, *Maintenance Administrator*

DIVISION OF LEGAL SERVICES
Monice Hagler, *City Attorney*
L. Kenneth McCown, Jr.,
  Deputy City Attorney

DIVISION OF MANAGEMENT AND INFORMATION SERVICES
John Hourican, *Director*
Claudia Shumpert, *Administrator*
Delia Bland, *Systems Information*
Tim Guntharp, *Micro Computers*

AUDITING SERVICES
Lillian Hite, *Director*

DIVISION OF ENGINEERING
James Collins, *City Engineer*
Paul Cheema, *Supervisor, Traffic Operations*
Larry Johnson, *Supervisor, City Sign Shop*

LENDERS TO THE EXHIBITION

WONDERS, The Memphis International Cultural Series, expresses its profound gratitude
to the following institutions and private collectors who have contributed
by their loans to the success of this exhibition

Their Imperial Highnesses Prince and Princess Napoleon
Administration Générale du Mobilier National, Paris
Archives Nationales, Paris
Jean Ariès, Paris
Bibliothèque Nationale, Paris
Bibliothèque Marmottan, Boulogne-Billancourt
Direction du Patrimoine, Paris
Fondation Dosne-Thiers, Musée Frédéric Masson, Paris
Fondation Napoléon, Paris
The Forbes Magazine Collection, New York
Baron Gourgaud, Paris
Olivier Le Fuel, Paris
Ministère des Affaires Etrangères, Paris
Musée Carnavalet, Paris
Musée Chaumet, Paris
Musée d'Art et d'Histoire, Palais Masséna, Nice
Musée de la Monnaie, Paris
Musée de l'Armée, Paris
Musée de l'Empéri, Salon-de-Provence
Musée de L'Île de France, Sceaux
Musée des Arts Décoratifs, Paris
Musée des Arts de la Mode et du Textile, Paris
Musée des Beaux-Arts, Nantes
Musée de Sens
Musée du Louvre, Département des Peintures, Paris
Musée du Louvre, Département des Objets d'Art, Paris
Musée Napoléon, Île d'Aix
Musée National de Céramique, Sèvres
Musée National de la Légion d'Honneur et des Ordres de Chevalerie, Paris
Musée National de la Maison Bonaparte, Ajaccio, Corsica
Musée National du Château de Fontainebleau
Musée National de Château du Malmaison
Musée National de l'Île d'Aix
Musée National du Château de Versailles
Musée Marmottan, Paris
Museum of Fine Arts, Boston
Napoleonmuseum, Arenenberg, Switzerland
National Archives, Washington, D.C.
National Gallery of Art, Washington, D.C.
National Museum of Natural History, Washington, D.C.
Capitaine de Vaisseau Philippe Olieu, Ajaccio, Corsica
Roger Prigent, New York
Van Cleef & Arpels, New York
Vatican Museums, State of Vatican City
Comte Charles-André Walewski, Paris
Wellington Museum, Apsley House, London

SPONSORS

PATRON
Edward W. Cook

SPONSORS
City of Memphis
Coca-Cola Bottling Company of Memphis
Federal Express Corporation
The Kroger Company
Naegele Outdoor Advertising, Inc.
Union Planters National Bank

OFFICIAL AIRLINE
Delta Air Lines, Inc.

CONTRIBUTORS

Alphagraphics
Larry Ashkenaz
Elizabeth Brinkerhoff
The Brownestone Hotel
The Commercial Appeal
Crowne Plaza Hotel
Embassy of The Republic of France
Embassy Suites Hotel
First Tennessee
George Falls
Gingiss Formalwear
Hospitality Sales and Marketing Association
George Jones
Proctor Jones
Junior League of Memphis
Lianna
Lithograph Printing Company
Memphis Area Transit Authority
Memphis Brooks Museum of Art
Memphis Business Journal
Memphis City Schools
Memphis Convention & Visitors Bureau
Memphis International Airport
Memphis State University
Memphis Queen Line
Metro Memphis Attractions Association
Metcalf Crump
Mississippi Press Association
The Napoleonic Society of America
National Council of Jewish Women
National Endowment for the Arts
National Geographic Society
Naval Air Station, Memphis
Loris J. Nierenberg, State Department
Northwest Airlink, Inc.
The Peabody Hotel
Gregory Peck
James H. Prentiss
Radisson Hotel
Schering-Plough
Seessel's Supermarkets
Shelby County Schools
Smith & Nephew Richards Inc.
Southwestern Wine & Liquor Company
K. Wallace Stuart, State Department
The Tri-State Defender Newspaper
Nick Vergos
Hiram Walker & Sons, Inc.
WHBQ-TV
WKNO-TV
WMC-TV
WREG-TV

A Statement from the
CURATOR OF THE EXHIBITION

Napoleon in Memphis! This extraordinary adventure, which started in 1989, has now become a reality. It is, in fact, the first exhibition organized in the United States which is exclusively dedicated to that most uncommon man, the Emperor Napoleon I. The exceptional scope and scale of this event explain why Their Imperial Highnesses, Prince and Princess Napoleon, have granted their patronage to the exhibition.

The determination of WONDERS and of the City of Memphis has provided a marvelous opportunity for international cooperation. The generous participation of more than fifty museums and private collectors in the United States and Europe has made it possible to bring together for the first time a large number of exceptional works of art, many of which have never previously crossed the Atlantic. It may be many years before such a collection of paintings, sculpture and precious objects can be assembled again. Our warmest thanks to all the lenders, who have agreed to give up their treasures for five long months. Such a grand exhibition would never have taken place without their full cooperation.

The great generosity of the City of Memphis found concrete expression in the restoration of the furniture and painted doors of the Council Chamber of the Musée National du Château de Malmaison. This room, which witnessed the signing of the treaty whereby the Louisiana Territory was returned to France, has been magnificently recreated in Memphis with its original furniture. The room's armchairs, stools and table covering have been sumptuously restored and reupholstered with new fabric and gold brocade.

Rarely have so many masterpieces which evoke the Emperor's private life, his military campaigns and the arts of the period been brought together at one time. Those fifteen short years were capital for the history of Europe, and if the military aspect of Napoleon's career is still the subject of debate, there is no criticism of his reforms in public administration, law, education, and commerce, many of which are still in effect in France and several other European countries.

I would like to take this opportunity to express my heartfelt thanks to the City of Memphis and to its mayor, Dr. W. W. Herenton, as well as to the resourceful and hard-working WONDERS team under the able direction of Jon Thompson. The WONDERS team members unfailingly accepted my suggestions and honored me with their complete confidence. I would be remiss, however, if I did not express my appreciation for the efficient and good-natured assistance of Thomas Michael Gunther, whose contributions were invaluable in bringing this exhibition to fruition.

It is my wish that this event might make it possible for our American friends to grow in their understanding of this very rich period in our history and to appreciate Napoleon even more for his exceptional qualities.

Bernard Chevallier
Chief Conservator of the
National Museum of the
Château of Malmaison

INTRODUCTION

The Atlantic Ocean may have played a key role in deciding the fate of Napoleon. Why? Revolutionary and imperial France had only one serious adversary—England. Though France succeeded in breaking up the continental coalition which London had formed with Austria, Prussia and Russia, it never conquered England. France simply did not have the necessary fleet to land its soldiers on English shores.

Initially, France sought to enlist other European sea powers as allies to compensate for its lack of naval power. Terrorized by the English fleet's bombing of Copenhagen, Denmark avoided such an alliance for a long time. During the *Directoire*, General Pichegru took over the Dutch navy, as the former United Provinces became a Batavian Republic allied with France. But Holland's naval power was on the wane. Spain was the source of again another disappointment as the days of the "Invincible Armada" were long past. At Trafalgar, the Spanish navy demonstrated how weak it had become. Nothing remained of the former might of Venice and Genoa.

The masterstroke of First Consul Bonaparte was to turn to the United States, a new country and a rising naval power. Previous alliances between the two countries had been weakened by a series of incidents, notably by acts of piracy committed by the French in the West Indies. As early as 1798, Talleyrand, Minister of Foreign Affairs during the *Directoire,* had laid the groundwork for a new Franco-American alliance, and it was his idea which was taken up again in 1800. The negotiations concerned the 1778 treaties between France and the United States, which the Americans considered to have been cancelled. These talks led to the Convention of Mortefontaine, signed on September 30, 1800, by Joseph Bonaparte, Fleurieu and Rodederer for the French and by Ellsworth, Davie and Vans Murray for the Americans.

The successful conclusion of the Convention was a serious blow to the English. Likely, it hastened England's decision to begin talks with France since a Paris-Washington axis already seemed formidable. Bonaparte confirmed the solidarity of the two countries as rivals of England:

> "The growth of the prosperity of the United States will never be a threat
> to France, and will even be very helpful in its struggle against England.
> The United States is destined by nature and circumstance to appropriate
> a share of Great Britain's sea trade and to reduce its influence as a world
> power."

Bonaparte continued to reinforce ties with the United States. He abandoned the idea of creating a colonial empire in the West Indies, after the failure of the Santo Domingo expedition. He then sold the Americans the Louisiana Territory, which had been returned to France by Spain. By these acts, Bonaparte strengthened his position against England. Nevertheless, the decisive blow was struck at Trafalgar, where, on October 21, 1805, the French admiral Villeneuve battled Nelson in a major defeat for Napoleon.

Unable to beat the English at sea, the new Emperor of the French began to fight an economic war. England's prosperity was based on exporting manufactured goods, produced at low prices. Its success was made possible by being technologically advanced over the rest of the continent, as well as on selling products to its colonies in India and the West Indies. If European markets were closed to British goods—and Napoleon could easily do so thanks to his conquests and the alliance concluded with the Czar at Tilsit in July 1807—England would be ruined and the pound would collapse.

The Continental Blockade was a key element in Napoleon's strategy. "I intend to conquer the sea with the might of the land," the Emperor was quoted as saying, an intention which was confirmed by the signing of the Berlin Decree on November 21, 1806. From then on, all trade between England and those parts of Europe controlled by Napoleon was forbidden. Yet, in the beginning, neutral countries, including the United States, were not concerned by these measures.

The French position espoused the American belief that "free ships made free goods," whereby, contraband excluded, a neutral flag covered the goods carried on the ship. As a naval power, Great Britain saw things differently. Since the Navigation Acts, the principal objective was to have all world trade handled by the English merchant marine on ships built and armed in England.

In the economic battle engendered by the Continental Blockade, England showed itself to be uncompromising. At first, England insisted on checking all the ships in the Atlantic, as illustrated by the *Chesapeake* incident in June 1807.

When war erupted in Europe in 1793 between Great Britain and revolutionary France, George Washington proclaimed the neutrality of the United States, and his successors had wanted to maintain this position. Nevertheless, the on-going struggle between Napoleon and England resulted in measures which proved intolerable: American trade was cut off in 1807 by the Embargo Act.

Not until the end of 1810 under President James Madison did the American government determine that the country's best interests placed it in the French camp. Yet, the United States did not declare war on England until 1812, and even then the Americans still refused to ally themselves with France. If the United States had gone to war earlier, say in 1809, it would have helped Napoleon by obliging the English, at a crucial moment in the Spanish War, to fight on another front. The economic crisis of 1810-1811 would also have had a greater impact on the English.

Thus help did not come from the United States as Napoleon had hoped when he addressed the Legislative Assembly on February 14, 1813:

> "America has taken up arms to make sure its flag is respected; the world's best wishes for success accompany it in this glorious struggle. If it finishes its fight by obliging the continent's enemies to recognize the principle that free ships make free goods and crews, and that neutral powers should not be subjected to paper blockades, in application of the Treaty of Utrecht, America will have earned the esteem of all peoples. Posterity will recount that the old world had lost its rights and that the new world had reconquered them."

Again in 1815, after having been beaten at Waterloo and exiled, Napoleon thought of seeking refuge in America. His reflections were in vain. On Saint Helena, he regretted not having done so:

> "America was our true refuge, from all points of view. It is a huge continent, where a special kind of freedom reigns. If you are melancholy, you can get in your carriage, ride a thousand leagues and enjoy being a simple traveller; there, you are everybody's equal; you lose yourself in the crowd as you like, with no problems, with your customs, your language, your religion."

Once again, in 1815, fate refused Napoleon the chance America represented.

For this reason alone, it is appropriate that the United States present Napoleon in the exhibition you are about to see, organized by WONDERS, The Memphis International Cultural Series. This time, America has taken the opportunity to welcome Napoleon, as yet another expression of Franco-American friendship, strengthening the bonds which were sealed by the blood shed on the battlefield in our century's two world wars.

Jean Tulard
Professor at the Sorbonne
President of the Institut Napoléon

Genealogy of the Bonaparte Family

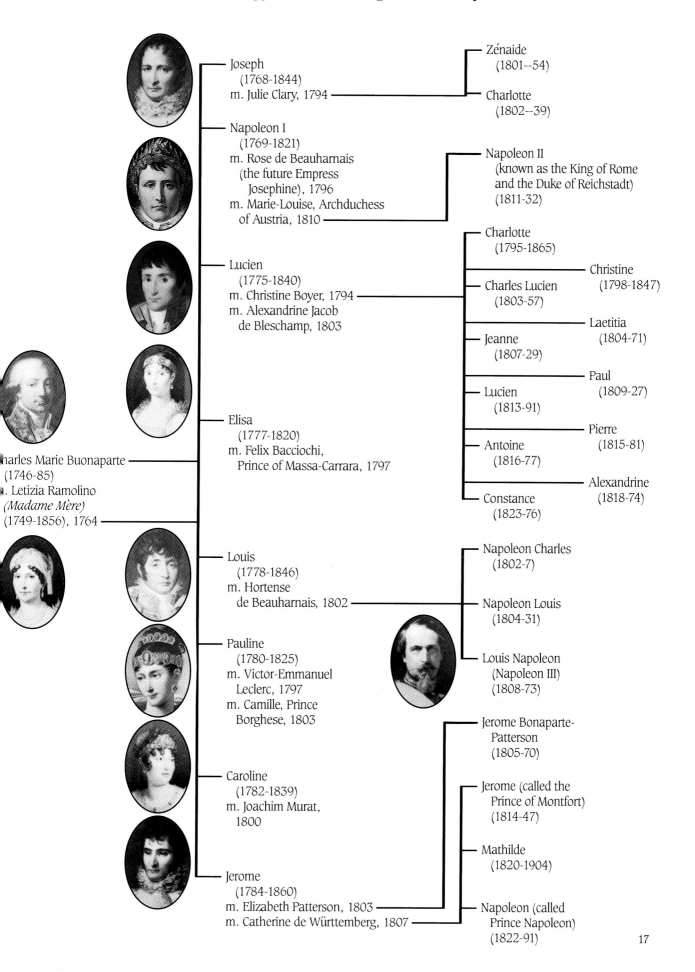

Joseph
(1768-1844)
m. Julie Clary, 1794

- Zénaide (1801--54)
- Charlotte (1802--39)

Napoleon I
(1769-1821)
m. Rose de Beauharnais
   (the future Empress
   Josephine), 1796
m. Marie-Louise, Archduchess
   of Austria, 1810

- Napoleon II
  (known as the King of Rome
  and the Duke of Reichstadt)
  (1811-32)

Lucien
(1775-1840)
m. Christine Boyer, 1794
m. Alexandrine Jacob
   de Bleschamp, 1803

- Charlotte (1795-1865)
- Charles Lucien (1803-57)
  - Christine (1798-1847)
- Jeanne (1807-29)
  - Laetitia (1804-71)
- Lucien (1813-91)
  - Paul (1809-27)
- Antoine (1816-77)
  - Pierre (1815-81)
- Constance (1823-76)
  - Alexandrine (1818-74)

Charles Marie Buonaparte
(1746-85)
m. Letizia Ramolino
(Madame Mère)
(1749-1856), 1764

Elisa
(1777-1820)
m. Felix Bacciochi,
   Prince of Massa-Carrara, 1797

Louis
(1778-1846)
m. Hortense
   de Beauharnais, 1802

- Napoleon Charles (1802-7)
- Napoleon Louis (1804-31)
- Louis Napoleon (Napoleon III) (1808-73)

Pauline
(1780-1825)
m. Victor-Emmanuel
   Leclerc, 1797
m. Camille, Prince
   Borghese, 1803

Caroline
(1782-1839)
m. Joachim Murat,
   1800

- Jerome Bonaparte-Patterson (1805-70)
- Jerome (called the Prince of Montfort) (1814-47)
- Mathilde (1820-1904)

Jerome
(1784-1860)
m. Elizabeth Patterson, 1803
m. Catherine de Württemberg, 1807

- Napoleon (called Prince Napoleon) (1822-91)

17

1769 *August 15*
Birth of Napoleon Bonaparte in Ajaccio, Corsica.

1774 Louis XVI becomes King of France.

1776 *July 4*
Declaration of Independence.

1779 *May 15*
Napoleon enters the royal military academy in Brienne near Troyes.

1783 *September 3*
The Treaty of Paris ends the Revolutionary War in the United States.

1784 *October 17*
Napoleon is admitted to the elite *Ecole Militaire* in Paris from which he graduates on October 28, 1785, with the rank of second lieutenant of artillery.

1785 *November 3*
Napoleon, age 16, is posted to Valence in the Rhone River Valley.

1786 *September*
Returns to Corsica for almost a year.

1788 *January-June*
Second trip to Corsica; stays six months.

June
With his regiment in Auxonne in Burgundy until September 1789.

1789 *April 30*
George Washington is inaugurated as first president of the United States.

July 14
Parisians storm the Bastille; absolute monarchy comes to an end as the *Ancien Régime* crumbles.

August 26
Declaration of the Rights of Man and of the Citizen.

September
Third trip to Corsica which lasts until February 1791; Napoleon sides with the revolutionary cause.

1791 *February-September*
With his regiment in Auxonne, then in Valence.

September
Fourth trip to Corsica; stays until May 1792.

September 14
The first French constitution; a constitutional monarchy is established.

1792 *April 20*
France declares war on Austria.

May-October
Bonaparte witnesses the storming of the Tuileries and the fall of the king in Paris.

September 21
Proclamation of France as a Republic with the official slogan "Liberty, Equality, Fraternity."

October
Fifth trip to Corsica. The Bonapartes are harassed by the Corsican patriots of General Paoli who accuse them of being too pro-French.

1793 *January 21*
King Louis XVI is guillotined; his widow Marie Antoinette will also be similarly executed.

February
England forms the first European coalition against France with Russia, Sardinia, Spain, Naples, Prussia, Austria, and the states of the Holy Empire.

June 13
After their house in Ajaccio is sacked by the Paolists, Napoleon and his family leave the island for Toulon in the south of France.

December 22
Bonaparte is raised to the rank of brigadier general for having distinguished himself during the siege of Toulon.

1794 *Ecole Polytechniques,* the world's first technical college, opens in Paris.

July 27
Fall of Robespierre ends the Reign of Terror.

August 9-20
Bonaparte, suspected of Jacobin sympathies, is imprisoned in Antibes.

1795 *June 13*
Bonaparte is named General of the Army of the West and is granted leave.

October
The *Directoire,* a five member board, is established to govern France; it lasts until 1799.

October 5
The government appoints Bonaparte to suppress any royalist insurrection against the Convention; he enters public life.

October 15
At the home of *Directoire* leader Barras, Napoleon meets the Citizen Rose de Beauharnais, a widow with two children who will become the Empress Josephine.

October 16
Supported by Barras, Bonaparte becomes Commander of the Army of the Interior.

1796 *March 2*
Bonaparte becomes Commander of the French army in Italy.

March 9
Wedding of Napoleon and Josephine in Paris.

March 11
Bonaparte joins his regiment and begins the Italian campaign against the Austrians.

May 10
The French win the Battle of Lodi.

June 1
Tennessee becomes the 16th U.S. state.

November 17
The French win the Battle of Arcole.

1797 *January 14*
The French defeat the Austrians in the Battle of Rivoli.

October 17
Treaty of Campo-Formio between France and Austria.

December 5
Bonaparte returns to Paris in triumph.

1798 *May 19*
Bonaparte departs for the Egyptian expedition.

July 2
The French take Alexandria.

July 21
The French defeat the Mameluke army and win the Battle of the Pyramids.

July 24
Bonaparte enters Cairo.

August 1
The French fleet is destroyed by Admiral Nelson off Aboukir.

1799 With England as the nucleus, the second coalition is formed by the Kingdom of the Two Sicilies, Turkey, Russia, and Austria.

March 7
The French take Jaffa.

March 19-May 10
Siege of Saint-Jean d'Acre, a seaport in what is today northwest Israel.

August 23
Worried by news from Paris, Bonaparte returns to France.

October 16
Bonaparte arrives in Paris.

November 9-10
Bonaparte initiates a *coup d'état* which enables him to become Consul of the Republic with Sieyes and Ducos; Talleyrand is appointed Foreign Minister.

December 13
A new constitution creates the Consular regime and Bonaparte announces that ''the Revolution is over.''

1800 Washington, D.C. is established as the new U.S. capital.

February 13
Creation of the *Banque de France*.

February 19
As First Consul, Napoleon takes up residence in the Tuileries Palace.

May 20
Second Italian Campaign; Bonaparte crosses the Alps by the Great Saint Bernard Pass.

June 14
The French defeat the Austrians in the Battle of Marengo.

1801 *February 9*
A peace agreement is signed with Austria at Lunéville.

July 15
Signing of the Concordat between the Holy See and the French Republic ends the religious schism.

December 24
Bonaparte escapes an attempt to assassinate him in Paris.

1802 *March 25*
The Treaty of Amiens is signed with England.

May 1
Reorganization of schools and creation of *lycées* (high schools).

May 19
Bonaparte creates the Legion of Honor.

August 4
Adoption of the new constitution; Bonaparte becomes Consul for life.

1803 *May 3*
Sale of the Louisiana Territory to the United States.

May 16
Violation of the Treaty of Amiens; war resumes with England.

1804 Lewis and Clark begin exploration of the northwestern area of what is now the United States.

January 29
Consular police thwart a royalist conspiracy against Bonaparte by Cadoudal.

March 21
Execution of the Duke d'Enghein.

May 18
Napoleon Bonaparte is proclaimed Emperor of the French; a new constitution creates an imperial monarchy which is really a dictatorial and military regime.

December 2
Coronation of Napoleon in Notre-Dame Cathedral in Paris.

1805 *March 17*
Napoleon is crowned King of Italy in Milan Cathedral.

April
Formation of the third coalition with England, Russia and Austria against France.

October 21
Admiral Nelson destroys the French fleet at Trafalgar.

December 2
The French win the Battle of Austerlitz.

December 26
Treaty of Pressburg with Austria.

1806 Fourth coalition with Russia, England, and Prussia against France.

March 15
Joachim Murat, the Emperor's brother-in-law, is named Grand Duke of Berg.

March 30
Joseph Bonaparte becomes King of Naples.

May 10
Creation of the imperial university.

June 5
Louis Bonaparte becomes King of Holland.

October 14
The French win the battles of Jena and Auerstadt.

October 27
Napoleon enters Berlin.

November 21
Continental Blockade begins which closes continental ports to British ships.

1807 *June 14*
Defeat of the Russians at Friedland.

July 7
Treaty of Tilsit between Czar Alexander I of Russia and the Emperor.

July 22
Creation of the Grandduchy of Warsaw.

August 16
Jerome Bonaparte becomes King of Westphalia.

November 30
Occupation of Portugal; dethroned Portuguese royal family flees to Brazil.

1808 *February 20*
Beginning of the French campaign in Spain under the command of Murat.

March 1
Creation of Empire nobility.

May 2
The population of Madrid revolts against the French occupying army.

June 4
Joseph becomes King of Spain; Murat replaces him in Naples.

1809 *April*
The fifth coalition is formed around England and Austria.

July 6
The French defeat the Austrians in the Battle of Wagram.

October 14
Peace of Vienna with Austria.

December 15
Napoleon and Josephine divorce.

1810 *April 2*
Religious wedding of Napoleon and Marie-Louise, Archduchess of Austria.

1811 *March 20*
Birth of Napoleon's son, the King of Rome.

1812 Louisiana becomes 18th U.S. state.

June 18
U.S. Congress declares war on Britain, thus beginning the War of 1812.

June 24
Napoleon crosses the Neman River and begins the disastrous Russian Campaign.

September 14
Napoleon enters Moscow, left in flames by fleeing Russians.

November 27
Retreating from Russia, the Great Army fights the Battle of Berezina.

December 18-19
Defeated, the Emperor returns to Paris, arriving during the night.

1813 The sixth coalition.

March 17
Prussia declares war on France.

June 21
Defeat of the French at Vitoria; Spain is lost.

August 12
Austria declares war on France.

October 15
Defeat at Leipzig, known as The Battle of the Nations; collapse of Napoleonic Germany.

November 16
Holland is lost; William of Orange returns.

1814 *January*
The French campaign; the coalition armies invade France.

March 30-31
Fall of Paris; the allies enter the capital.

April 2
The Empress Marie-Louise and the King of Rome flee to Blois; the Senate proclaims the fall of Napoleon.

April 4
Abdication of the Emperor; royal authority is re-established under the Bourbons; return to a constitutional monarchy.

April 6
Louis XVIII, brother of Louis XVI, is proclaimed King of France.

April 20
Napoleon's farewell at Fontainebleau.

May 4
Napoleon is exiled to Elba (an island off the northwest coast of Italy); Marie-Louise and the King of Rome go to Vienna.

May 29
Death of the Empress Josephine at the Château of Malmaison.

1815 *March 1*
The Emperor returns to France, landing in the Golfe Juan.

March 7
The army rallies to Napoleon.

March 20
Louis XVIII flees to Ghent, Belgium; in Paris, Napoleon assumes reign for what is known as ''The Hundred Days.''

April 22
Adoption of the Additional Act to the Constitutions of the Empire, which establishes an ephemeral liberal Empire.

June 18
Wellington defeats Napoleon at Waterloo.

June 22
Napoleon abdicates again; second restoration.

July 15
Having taken refuge on the Île d'Aix, the Emperor surrenders to the English.

October 16
Napoleon is exiled to Saint Helena, a barren island in the South Atlantic.

1821 *May 5*
Death of Napoleon.

1832 *July 22*
Death, in Vienna, of Napoleon's son, the King of Rome, who became the Duke of Reichstadt in 1816.

1840 *May*
The English government agrees to allow the Emperor's ashes to be returned to France.

July 7
Departure of the Saint Helena expedition under the command of the Prince de Joinville, the son of King Louis-Philippe I.

October 15
Napoleon's body is exhumed.

October 18
The imperial bier, called the *Retour des Cendres*, begins its return and arrives December 2.

December 15
Napoleon's body is placed in the *Invalides* in compliance with his final wishes.

1847 *December 17*
Death of the Empress Marie-Louise, who was made reigning Duchess of Parma by the Congress of Vienna in 1815.

1852 *December 2*
Second Empire; Prince Louis-Napoleon Bonaparte, Napoleon's nephew, is proclaimed Emperor of the French under the name Napoleon III.

1861 Completion of Napoleon's tomb under the dome of the *Invalides*.

1870 *September 4*
Fall of the Second Empire; return to a republican form of government.

December 15
1940 Adolph Hitler returns the ashes of the Duke of Reichstadt (Napoleon's son) to France.

Coronation Port
Napoleon as King of
(cat. no. 79,

BACKGROUND AND NAPOLEON'S YOUTH
1769 - 1793

*I sealed the yawning abyss of anarchy, and thwarted chaos. I cleansed
the Revolution, raised up peoples and strengthened monarchy. I inspired
all forms of ambition, rewarded merit on every occasion, and stretched
the bounds of fame. All that surely amounts to something! On what
grounds could I be accused that would make it impossible for any historian
to defend me? My intentions, perhaps? He will be able to clear me. My
despotism? He can prove that dictatorship was necessary. Will people
say I tied the hands of freedom? He can show that license, anarchy and
major upheaval were still a threat. Will I be accused of loving war too
much? He will prove that I was always only defending myself. Of wanting
to set up a universal monarchy? He will demonstrate that it was the for-
tuitous result of circumstances, that it was our enemies themselves who
led me down that path step by step. My ambition? No doubt he will find
that I had a good measure of such, but of the noblest and highest sort
that might ever have existed—the ambition to establish and consecrate
at long last the empire of reason and the full exercise, the complete enjoy-
ment of all human faculties! And here the historian may find himself
forced to regret that the goals of such ambition were never reached, that
such aims were never accomplished. [After several minutes of silence
and reflection, the Emperor added,] My dear friend, here, in a few
words, you have my full story.*

Napoleon Bonaparte
Mémorial de Sainte-Hélène, 1823
Conversation with General Las Cases, Saint Helena,
May 1, 1816

Although the island of Corsica had been controlled by the Republic of Genoa since the
thirteenth century, its strategic location in the Mediterranean, off both the Italian and
French coasts, made other nations covet this prize possession. On May 15, 1768, according
to the provisions of the Treaty of Versailles, Genoa ceded to France its rights to the island
which is little more than a huge shipwrecked mountain.

It was, therefore, one of those remarkable historical coincidences that the birth of
Napoleon Bonaparte in Ajaccio on August 15, 1769, occurred while the troops of Louis XV
were taking possession of Corsica. Rapidly, in order to foster the development of a French
faction, the King sought to gain the support of the island's nobles, whom he incorporated
into the kingdom's established aristocracy. Napoleon's family, though originally from
Tuscany, had been in Ajaccio since the fifteenth century. On September 13, 1771, Charles
Buonaparte, the father of the future emperor, had his family officially declared ''nobles
whose nobility can be proven to be more than 200 years old.'' (Napoleon adopted the
French-influenced spelling of his last name, Bonaparte, after becoming a captain in
the French army.)

Born in 1746, Charles joined the French camp, basically because his rather precarious
financial situation left him little choice. In 1764, he married Letizia Ramolino, the fifteen-year-
old daughter of a noble family from Lombardy that had arrived in Ajaccio in the sixteenth
century. The following year, Letizia, officially known as *Madame Mère* during the Empire,
gave birth to her first son, who died at a very young age.

Of the twelve children Letizia bore before her husband's premature death in 1785,
eight survived to play a role in the imperial epic—Joseph, born in 1768 (the eldest
Bonaparte child), King of Naples, and later of Spain, the acknowledged head of the family

after the death of their father; Napoleon, born in 1769; Lucien, Prince of Canino, born in 1775; Elisa, Grand Duchess of Tuscany, born in 1777; Louis, King of Holland, born in 1778; Pauline, the wife of Prince Borghese, born in 1780; Caroline, Grand Duchess of Berg and Cleves, later Queen of Naples, born in 1782; and finally Jerome, King of Westphalia, born in 1784, who first married Elizabeth Patterson, the daughter of a wealthy Baltimore tradesman.

The Buonapartes took advantage of the privileges that their status as French aristocrats afforded them. In 1777, Charles obtained a royal scholarship for Napoleon to the Royal Military Academy in Brienne (Champagne). Napoleon was a student in Brienne until October 1784, when he was admitted to Paris' prestigious military college, the *Ecole Militaire,* founded by Louis XV to train young men to be both officers and gentlemen.

Napoleon's formative years in these royal academies appear to have been solitary, though studious, interrupted only by his father's death in Montpellier on February 24, 1785. Attaining the rank of second lieutenant of artillery in the La Fère regiment helped Napoleon forget his loss and was a justifiable source of pride, all the more so since he was the first Corsican to graduate from the *Ecole Militaire*. He began his career as a soldier, pursuing his ambition until that fateful evening at Waterloo on June 15, 1815.

In November 1785, Napoleon left Paris for the Rhone River Valley, where his regiment was stationed in Valence. To break the boredom and monotony of garrison life in peacetime, he read voraciously, determined to complete his education. He devoured books on history, natural history and geography. Tales of antiquity fascinated him. He discovered the history of Egypt and recorded the measurements of the pyramids, studied the great empires—Athens, Rome and Byzantium—and dreamed of the conquests of Alexander and Hannibal. He investigated the modern forms of government introduced by the Turks, the Arabs and the Venetian Republic. He studied the history of England, commented upon France's past and wrote about royal authority. He drew up a list of English possessions in America, Asia and Africa (noting among them: "Saint Helena, a small island!"). Yet, even if this earnest, idealistic and melancholy young officer frequently dreamed of the future, glimpses could already be seen of the cold, calculating and brilliant general he would become.

In 1789, however, Napoleon did not see the gathering storm that was about to break. The financial crisis of the *Ancien Régime* inevitably led to the downfall of the absolute monarchy. France's support of the American cause during the War of Independence cost more than the Royal Treasury could afford, making it necessary to borrow money since it was impossible to raise taxes. The imminent specter of bankruptcy finally obliged Louis XVI to convoke a meeting in May 1789 of the *Etats Généraux,* which included the elected representatives of the three orders of the realm—nobility, clergy and commoners. The determination of the deputies of the Third Estate, which represented the people, to demand fiscal equality was met by the absolute and uncompromising refusal of the privileged classes—the nobles and the clergy, who were supported by the King.

The final break came on June 21, when the *Etats Généraux* declared themselves a National Assembly and affirmed the higher principle of the sovereignty of the Nation. The Revolution had begun, and Louis XVI could not stop the impetus. On July 14, 1789, in defiance of royal power, the population of Paris stormed the Bastille, a government prison which was partly closed, but which symbolized the arbitrary justice of the absolute monarchy. During the nights of August 4 and 5, the National Assembly abolished all privileges, and on August 26, it adopted the Declaration of Human and Citizen Rights, inspired by the American Declaration of Independence. Traditional social hierarchy was abolished, absolutism was overthrown, and freedom and equality were finally won.

The events in Paris seemed to leave Napoleon indifferent. Having obtained leave in mid-August, he left the continent for Ajaccio. Nothing had changed in Corsica, for the royal governor had not informed the islanders about the Revolution. At the request of his fellow Corsicans, Napoleon wrote the National Assembly to complain of the attitude of the King's representative. "You who are the protectors of freedom," he wrote, "deign to pay us some attention from time to time, for we were formerly its most zealous defenders." Napoleon had anchored his native island firmly in the revolutionary camp.

In 1791, Napoleon went back to his regiment in Valence, and then returned to Ajaccio at the end of the year. By the summer of 1792, he was in Paris on business, and the capital was in an uproar. France had declared war on Austria on April 20, 1792, and on England on February 1, 1793. Prussia, soon followed by the German states, Russia, Spain, Naples, and Sardinia, joined the coalition against the French. Louis XVI tried in vain to thwart the Revolution, but his attempt to flee abroad had left him suspected of treason.

House in Which Napoleon Was Born
(cat. no. 16, p. 51).

Rival political factions were at each other's throats. There was utter chaos. On August 10, a mob attacked the Tuileries Palace, where the King and his family were in residence, to demand that the King be handed over to the people for trial. The brave Royal Guard, made up of Swiss soldiers, was massacred with no quarter given. As a witness to these events, Napoleon was deeply impressed by what he saw. Years later, on Saint Helena, he recalled: "Never have any of my battlefields seemed to be strewn with so many slain soldiers as there were Swiss guards who died that day." On the evening of August 10, the monarchy was overthrown. The French Republic, "one and indivisible," was proclaimed on September 25.

Meanwhile, in Napoleon's homeland, those who favored joining the new Republic, led by the Bonapartes, confronted those who dreamed of a free and independent Corsica. In June 1793, after their house in Ajaccio was looted, Napoleon and his family decided it was wiser to go to the mainland. They landed in Toulon on June 13 and found southern France in determined rebellion. Napoleon was immediately requisitioned to serve in the Republican army since the southwestern and southeastern provinces had revolted against Paris. Having seceded from the Republic, they refused to obey any orders from the capital. The Revolution found itself in serious straits during that summer of 1793. The Austro-Prussian armies had trampled France's borders, and civil war raged within the country. Toulon surrendered to the English fleet, and Marseille federalists, supported by their Lyon counterparts, controlled the whole Rhone Valley.

Under the orders of General Carteaux, a former court painter who became a commanding Officer in the Revolution, Napoleon took part in the siege of Toulon, which had to be wrested from the English. In the midst of the fighting, the brother of Robespierre, who would inspire the Terror, noticed how well the intrepid and untiring artillery captain commanded his batteries. After the enemy troops had hastily reboarded their ships on September 22, the evening of the first assault, Napoleon was named brigadier general in recognition of his courage and valor. He won a reputation there, but he also caught a terrible skin disease which gave him the olive complexion and leanness so often noticeable in his early portraits.

THE YOUNG GENERAL PROVES HIMSELF
1793 - 1799

The day after the fall of Robespierre (July 27, 1794), Napoleon was arrested since he was suspected of harboring Jacobin sympathies. Imprisoned in Antibes (August 9), he was, however, soon cleared of all charges (August 20). Rather than depart for his assignment with the army in Vendée, Napoleon preferred to take leave and return to Paris.

To avoid the risk of another dictatorship, a new constitution, adopted in 1795, entrusted executive power to a five-member committee called the *Directoire*. In October, the royalist insurrection took a more dramatic turn. The government assigned Barras, an influential member of the *Directoire*, the task of re-establishing law and order and placed all available generals under his authority. When the royalist uprising was put down on 13 *Vendémiaire* (October 5), Napoleon was propelled to the front of the political scene. Barras chose Napoleon as second-in-command of the Army of the Interior on October 8 and named

him commander-in-chief on October 26. During this time, Napoleon met Rose de Beauharnais, the future Empress Josephine, at the home of Barras. She was the widow of a general who had been guillotined during the Reign of Terror and the mother of two children, Eugène and Hortense. Although Napoleon first courted her without any real conviction, he soon fell madly in love, and they married on March 9, 1796, without even informing his family.

By 1795, fighting had stopped between France and most of her enemies. The only unresolved conflicts were with England on the seas and on land with Austria, which was supported by the southern German states and Italian princes such as the King of Piedmont-Sardinia. In 1796, there was a serious attempt to reach a general peace agreement. Persuaded that France could only defeat England by winning on the continent, Napoleon advised attacking Austria, London's ally, by undertaking a military offensive in northern Italy. He convinced the *Directoire* of his plan, and was named commander of the army of Italy on March 2, 1796. Napoleon knew the advantage to be gained by acting quickly. By

Portraits of Josephine rarely show her smiling as she was self-conscious about her poor teeth. Pierre-Paul Prud'hon used pastels to create this early and informal portrait of the future Empress.

March 26, he was ready to move, and his lightning offensive took the enemy by surprise. In just eighteen days (April 10-28), he defeated the Sardinian army, pushed back the Austrians, won six battles, and forced the King of Sardinia to withdraw from the allied coalition against France. After eliminating Piedmont, Napoleon concentrated on Austria. On May 10, the French smashed the Austrian rear-guard at Lodi. On the sixteenth, they entered Milan. The Austrians had to evacuate Lombardy rapidly, and they retreated to Mantua. With Napoleon occupying Lombardy, the Dukes of Parma and Modena, the King of Naples and the Pope were left with no option but to surrender to the French (May-June 1796). While Napoleon's troops were beginning to feel the strain of the campaign, a superior force made up of about 60,000 reinforcements arrived from Austria. Napoleon, nevertheless, attacked the Austrians in the swamps of Arcole (November 15-17) and defeated them at Rivoli (January 14, 1797). Mantua surrendered on February 2. The campaign was over. Yet capitalizing on this victory, Napoleon moved into Austria, marching on Vienna to force Emperor Francis II to sue for peace. The armistice was signed on March 31. After preliminary negotiations in Leoben on April 18, 1797, the Treaty of Campo-Formio was signed on October 17.

General Napoleon Bonaparte at the Bridge of Arcole (cat. No. 20, p. 54).

The Italian Campaign made France aware of its military might and convinced Napoleon of his lofty ambition. His fame was at its zenith. He had negotiated with the enemy without paying the slightest attention to the *Directoire* which, once all was said and done, could only concur. The government had no choice but to lavish honors on the hero of the Italian Campaign. In fact, the Treaty of Campo-Formio re-established peace in Europe. France had defeated Austria, recovered its natural frontiers, and consolidated its hold on Italy. Only England held out. From this point on, it was the avowed enemy, the adversary that had to be crushed at any cost.

The *Directoire* argued for an invasion of England, but Napoleon had a much more ambitious plan, which he thought would put a definite end to the supremacy of proud

Britain. For many months, he had been dreaming of the East. To destroy England, he calculated, France must conquer Egypt, a province of the Ottoman Empire, and then move on to India, from which the English would be expelled. The time was right, since Sultan Selim III no longer controlled Egypt, which had fallen into the hands of the Mamelukes and the beys who commanded them.

Assured of the support of Talleyrand, the Minister of Foreign Affairs, Napoleon convinced the five members of the *Directoire* to agree to his plan. The government was, perhaps, even relieved to see this general who had become dangerously popular leave France to undertake a distant campaign. Napoleon sailed from Toulon on May 19, 1798, with 54,000 men and 280 ships. He was accompanied by some of the Republic's most brilliant officers—Berthier, Murat, Lannes, Kléber, and Desaix. Artists and scientists were also included in the expeditionary force that set out to conquer Egypt.

On its way across the Mediterranean, the French fleet captured Malta on June 9. It reached Alexandria on July 1, having eluded the pursuing English fleet, under the command of Admiral Nelson. The Mamelukes, who had rebelled, were Napoleon's enemy. By July 7, he was fighting in the desert and moving up the Nile toward Cairo. On July 21, he engaged the Mameluke army at Gaza. Before the battle, Napoleon harangued his troops. Pointing to the pyramids, he told them: "Soldiers, forty centuries of history are watching you." Victory gave him control of the Egyptian capital, but his luck was running out. On August 1, Nelson destroyed the French fleet at Aboukir. Cut off from his supply base, Napoleon became a prisoner in Egypt. Meanwhile, as Desaix was successfully waging war in upper Egypt, Napoleon, who referred to himself as the "worthy son of the Prophet," was putting his stamp on the Delta region. The Sultan finally reacted, however, and, in February 1799, sent two armies after Napoleon—one by sea to Alexandria with the support of the English and the other by land from Syria. Napoleon, with barely 12,000 men, decided to advance into Palestine to engage the 500,000 warriors of the powerful Turkish army.

On February 24, 1799, he reached Gaza; on March 7, he stormed the fortified port of Jaffa where the plague struck many of his soldiers. On March 19, he attacked Saint John of Acre, but was not able to capture the city. On May 10, he finally raised the siege, left Syria and retreated to Cairo with the survivors of an army decimated by epidemics. Regrouping his troops, Napoleon defeated the 18,000 janissaries of the second Turkish army entrenched in Aboukir on July 25, pushing them to the coast.

The situation had turned to his advantage. The country's borders were secured, the Mamelukes defeated and the population under control. Yet, the news from France was infinitely more alarming and convinced Napoleon he should return to Paris immediately. The *Directoire* had ordered the occupation of the Papal States and Switzerland. Again, Europe was at war. Napoleon expressed his aggravation and his ambition to one of his officers: "I'll get rid of that bunch of lawyers who pay us no heed and who are incapable of governing the Republic, and then I'll take over." He announced to his soldiers that he was handing command over to General Kléber and that they would soon have news of him. On August 23, 1799, he secretly set sail for France. Reports of his arrival in Fréjus on October 9 spread quickly throughout the population.

In Paris, Napoleon found the government in desperate straits. Complete control was his for the taking, and with the help of Talleyrand and Father Sieyes, he organized a *coup d'état* on 18 *Brumaire* (November 9, 1799). Named First Consul of the Republic, Napoleon declared that the Revolution was over.

Much later, Napoleon revealed that it was not until after the Battle of the Pyramids that the scope of his ambition became clear to him: "Then I really knew that my wildest dreams could come true." Napoleon was on his way to becoming Emperor.

Bonaparte as First Consul (cat. no. 32, p. 62).

THE FIRST CONSUL
1800 - 1804

In an attempt to end hostilities with England and Austria, Bonaparte had made peace overtures in December 1799. They were rejected, and the First Consul decided to impose his will by force. In May 1800, he assisted Italy which was again threatened by the coalition of allies against France. With surprising daring, he moved his troops across the Alps by way of the Great Saint Bernard Pass. On June 9, he was in Milan, and on the fourteenth, he crushed the Austrians at Marengo. England, exhausted by seven years of incessant warfare, finally agreed to lay down arms. The signing of the Treaty of Lunéville with the Austrian Emperor Francis II on February 9, 1801, and of the Treaty of Amiens with London on March 27, 1802, brought peace to the continent, although it would be of short duration.

Meanwhile, half a world away, new opportunities blossomed. In order not to compromise these delicately crafted arrangements, Bonaparte abandoned the idea of taking possession of Louisiana. Spain had returned the territory to France according to terms of a treaty which the two countries officially ratified in the Council Chamber of Malmaison on October 2, 1801. The First Consul was aware of President Jefferson's determination to defend American territory against any foreign power that might have designs on New Orleans. Bonaparte thought it wiser to come to an agreement with "this burgeoning power," as he called the United States. On April 30, 1803, Louisiana was sold to the Americans for 60 million francs, plus 20 million francs to cover indemnities (for a total of approximately $15,000,000).

To the world, France appeared to have come out of the Revolution a stronger nation. However, it had been seriously weakened domestically by six years of fierce fighting for power among the different political factions. Thus, Bonaparte's first task was to re-establish peace within the country. The First Consul confirmed his extraordinary skill as an organizer and statesman. "To deal with public, administrative and military affairs," he used to say, "one must have strength of character, the power to analyze in depth and the ability to concentrate for long periods of time without tiring."

Pursuing a skillful policy of appeasement, Bonaparte worked to re-create national unity, facilitating the return of the *émigrés*, encouraging the royalists to support the Consulate, and out-maneuvering the leaders of the Chouan rebellion (January 1800). But for the country to be at peace, it was necessary to end the schism which had torn the Church apart since 1789 and was still far from being settled. After a year of difficult negotiations, periodically on the point of being broken off and often interrupted, a Concordat

With the purchase of the Louisiana Territory, the United States doubled in size. The treaty extended the western U.S. boundary from the Mississippi River to the Rocky Mountains. Part or all of 15 states were later formed from the region.

Paul Delarouce. *Bonaparte Crosses the Alps,* 1848.

Though one of Napoleon's most famous portraits shows him astride a horse as he
crossed the Alps (cat. no. 38, p. 66), Napoleon actually rode a more sure-footed
mule. This painting by Paul Delarouche depicts the hazardous nine-day journey as
it actually occurred. A Swiss guide safely led Napoleon's army over the treacherous
mountains, and in appreciation, Napoleon awarded the guide a small farm and cottage.

was finally signed on July 15, 1801, between France and the Holy See. By its terms, Pius
VII relinquished the Church's claim to confiscated ecclesiastical property—something which
amounted to de facto recognition of the French Republic by Rome, and Bonaparte declared
Catholicism the "religion of the majority of the French," without giving up the principle of
religious pluralism. In this way, the First Consul confirmed his authority over a Church
whose clergy and people now unequivocally owed him allegiance. Religious harmony was
the essential corollary to the peace of the nation. It consecrated the success of the policy
of national reconciliation introduced by the First Consul.

As he was pacifying the country's warring factions, Bonaparte simultaneously worked
to bring about the political, administrative and social reorganization of France. At the height
of his popularity, which he adroitly knew how to turn to his advantage, he began by centraliz-
ing government administrative services (February 1800). He then addressed the nation's
finances, restoring creditworthiness and the currency while supporting the creation of the
Banque de France (February 1800). He overhauled the educational system, modeling it on
military training. The first *lycées* were established in May 1802 to train future government
employees who would be both qualified and reliable, and the French university system was
established in 1808. Bonaparte was particularly determined to reform French civil law, a
project that had been around since Louis XIV. This vast and ambitious undertaking, begun

in July 1800, was actively supported by the First Consul himself, who multiplied contacts with legal authorities to hurry the project along. The new Civil Code, later called the Napoleonic Code, became law on March 21, 1804. With modifications, it remains the civil code of France today, and many regard it as Napoleon's most lasting achievement.

According to Portalis, one of the members of the drafting committee, ''a civil code is a set of laws intended to govern and define the relations of sociability, family and interest existing among men who belong to the same political system.'' This mammoth under- taking, with its 2,281 articles, confirmed the triumph of the social conquests of the bourgeois Revolution—the cohesion of the family was restored by placing the wife and children under the authority of the father; the absolute right to property was reaffirmed; and the freedom of will that makes man his own master was officially recognized.

Bonaparte took advantage of the peace he had restored to increase his own powers. Proclaimed First Consul for life in August 1802, he had a new constitution adopted which gave him the right to designate his successor. A return to a monarchial regime was not far off. The Tuileries, the former palace of the French kings, became the official residence of the head of state. A forerunner of a consular court took shape around Josephine, and the Legion of Honor, a new form of patriciate, was created in May 1802, because, according to Bonaparte himself, ''it is with baubles that men are led.''

But the more the political scene moved ostensibly away from republican ideals, the more worried the royalists became, since they still nursed a vain hope that the monarchy would be re-established. Hostilities were renewed between England and France in 1803, after the Treaty of Amiens was violated. Several royalists who had taken refuge in London took advantage of the rift to hatch a plot against the First Consul with the blessing of the English. Yet the conspiracy of Cadoudal came to nought in October because of an untimely denunciation. Arrested and questioned, the conspirators confessed that they had acted for a French prince. The fact that Louis de Bourbon-Condé, Duke of Enghien and the cousin of Louis XVI, happened to be in the German Duchy of Baden at the time proved to Bonaparte that he was the guilty party. Shrouded in utmost secrecy, Bonaparte's police kidnapped the prince on March 15, 1804, brought him back to Paris, and, after a mock trial, executed him in the trenches of the Château of Vincennes near Paris. The assassination of the prince precipitated a definitive break with the royalists. There was no further obstacle between Bonaparte and the throne. On May 18, 1804, the Senate proclaimed Napoleon Emperor of the French and Josephine became his Empress.

NAPOLEON EMPEROR
1804

With the creation of the Napoleonic Empire, Napoleon established himself as the successor of Charlemagne, from whom he borrowed the eagle with spread wings to decorate his standards. From that point on, the new Emperor was on equal footing with the Emperors of Germany and Russia. The official Coronation of Napoleon as Emperor in December 1804 provided the occasion for sumptuous festivities of unprecedented splendor.

The Pope, invited to attend in order to ''give the ceremony a pre-eminently religious character,'' resigned himself to travelling to Paris. By agreeing to participate, Pius VII hoped to obtain several favors for the Papal States from Napoleon. On December 2, a cold, yet sunny, winter's day, the Emperor and the Empress, cloaked in velvet and ermine, were crowned under the golden tapestries that decorated the Cathedral of Notre-Dame. On December 5, on the Champ-de-Mars in Paris, Napoleon presented the army with its flags. To the soldiers who, in spite of the snow, paraded in front of him, he declared: ''These eagles will always be your rallying point. They will be wherever your Emperor decides they are necessary to defend his throne and his people.'' Several months later on May 26, 1805, in Milan, Napoleon crowned himself King of Italy, placing the traditional iron crown on his

Jacques Louis David.
Preliminary Sketch for The Consecration of Emperor Napoleon and the Coronation of the Empress Josephine at Notre-Dame.

Artist Jacques Louis David first sketched this scene of Napoleon crowning himself before embarking on his massive 30 foot (9.14 m.) canvas which depicts Napoleon crowning Josephine. By choosing to crown himself, Napoleon signalled to the world that he was not subservient to Pope Pius VII or the Church of Rome.

Jacques Louis David. *The Consecration of Emperor Napoleon and the Coronation of the Empress Josephine at Notre Dame,* 1806-1807.

Napoleon sought to keep his family near him throughout his career, and his Coronation was no exception. Among those represented in David's painting are 1) Napoleon; 2) his mother who interestingly chose not to attend in order to be with her son Lucien in Rome who was then in disfavor with Napoleon [the Emperor later ordered David to include his mother in the painting]; 3) Josephine; 4) Pope Pius VII; 5) Joseph Bonaparte; 6) and his wife, Julie Clary; 7) Louis Bonaparte; 8) and his wife, Hortense who was Josephine's daughter; 9) Caroline Bonaparte; 10) and her husband, General Murat; 11) Pauline Bonaparte; 12) Elisa Bonaparte; 13) Eugène de Beauharnais, son of Josephine; 14) the artist David.

own head. The advent of a new dynasty was celebrated throughout Paris and the French provinces.

After 1804, Napoleon was determined to re-establish an aristocracy, whose wealth and influence would be linked to the imperial government. But it was not until 1808, when he was at the height of his power, that he created a functional nobility, granting hereditary titles under certain conditions to individuals rather than to families. It was not a question of reinstating the kind of nobility that had existed in the *Ancien Régime*, but rather to establish a "titled class" which would bring together men from all horizons who had distinguished themselves by the quality of the services they rendered to the Napoleonic dynasty.

Innocent-Louis Goubaud. *A Delegation from the Roman Senate Pays Its Respects to Napoleon in the Throne Room of the Tuileries Palace, November 16, 1809.*

Since there is no power without public show, royal protocol was reinstated, and the Court of Louis XVI served as a model for palace life under the Emperor and the Empress. "I had to create an external facade," Napoleon said later, "and assume a serious demeanor, or more succinctly put, an etiquette; otherwise, people would have been slapping me on the back whenever they saw me." The formal etiquette of the imperial palaces, published in 1806, regulated every moment of the lives of the sovereigns, including the attribution of apartments, the ceremonial rituals that governed meals, rising, going to bed, religious services, balls, concerts, and even court funerals. Even though she had not been born to rule, Josephine accepted these constraints with ease, elegance, and perhaps even a slight twinge of pleasure. As for Napoleon, he did his best to play the part, although, as he himself admitted, ''It is harder than one thinks to speak to a crowd of people and not say anything, to meet a multitude of people of whom nine out of ten are unknown to you.''

The obligations bound up with the representation of power forced the Emperor to lead a double life—one public, in the Great Apartments of the imperial palaces, the other private, protected from inquisitive eyes behind the walls of his inner sanctuary. There, Napoleon was more like himself. He reassumed his familiar habits of constant work and almost obsessive tidiness. Locked in his study for days at a time when he was not at war, he spent long hours dictating innumerable letters, notes, and projects. He worked individually with his ministers, the Prince Archchancellor Cambacérès or the Archtreasurer Lebrun, with the Secretary of State Maret, Duke of Bassano. One morning, as he was getting up and cutting his nails, he said, ''I was born and built for work, not for digging. I have not yet encountered the limit of my capacity for work.''

Extremely respectful of moral decorum and convinced that power depends as much on the grandeur of a regime as on its strength, the Emperor showered gifts and favors on Josephine, his brothers and sisters who had by now become princes and princesses, as well as on the high dignitaries of the realm. He wanted his court to be sumptuous; it was splendid, ceremonial and sad all at the same time. Court etiquette, modeled on that of Versailles, crushed the receptions under waves of intimidating solemnity. Yet even if life at the Tuileries or at Saint Cloud was not very entertaining, the court's standard of living required enormous investments which boosted French industry and encouraged the arts.

In fact, as Napoleon once told Vivant Denon, the most important thing was grandeur, for, he added, what is grand is beautiful. Art during the Empire easily became monumental and revealed an attachment to aesthetic options inspired by Greco-Roman, or even Egyptian, antiquity. Neoclassicism triumphed everywhere—in painting with David and his students, in sculpture with Chaudet and Canova, and in architecture with Percier and Fontaine, who were the true instigators of the Empire style along with David.

The decorative arts did not escape their influence. Cabinet-makers built solid mahogany furniture with straight lines and right angles, decorated the arms of armchairs with sphinxes' heads, and designed camp-stools to look like the curule chairs of the ancient Romans. With numerous orders from the imperial household, Parisian goldsmiths again expanded operations. By purchasing new silverware in vast quantities for the imperial palaces (Louis XVI's had been melted down during the Revolution), Napoleon supported the activities of an old and honorable trade. For the Emperor's Coronation, the City of Paris ordered a magnificent table service in vermeil, made up of not less than 1,067 pieces, from the famous goldsmith Henri August. In the year 1811 alone, Biennais delivered nine major shipments of silver and vermeil tableware for the imperial palaces. As for Josephine, she had an almost fanatical passion for gold-plate and jewelry,

Napoleon and Josephine spent many of their most treasured moments at Château of Malmaison. As part of the divorce decree, Josephine was allowed to continue residing there until her death in 1814.

as well as for dresses. At her death, in 1814, the coffers at Malmaison overflowed with three million francs worth of jewels, perhaps the largest private collection ever assembled by a sovereign. Luxury goods made in Paris were exported to all the European courts. The Empress Maria Feodorovna, the mother of Czar Alexander the First, as well as the King of Bavaria, Maximilian-Joseph, ordered impressive table sets in vermeil, engraved with their coats of arms, from Biennais and Odiot.

Interior decoration was also influenced by ancient Rome, when it was not inspired by more blatantly military themes, as symbols of war rivaled with mythological themes. This style, however, had little to do with the personal tastes of the Emperor, who was not confident of his ability to make judgments about artistic matters. Yet, if Napoleon hesitated to impose his own tastes, he wanted art to serve his prestige. Official art was nourished by Napoleonic propaganda. A decree of 1806, for example, obliged artists to represent, in their future works, ''the Emperor haranguing the second army at Augsburg,'' and ''the Austrian prisoners of war, leaving Ulm and marching before His Majesty.'' By the same token, the monuments built during this period in Paris, such as the Arc of Carrousel and the Vendôme Column, celebrated the glory of the Emperor and his soldiers. Napoleon also planned to remodel the capital to make it ''the most beautiful city that could be.'' Paris would be covered with arcades and colonnades. The Emperor dreamt of a triumphal avenue which would extend from the Temple of Glory at the Madeleine to a Temple of Peace which would be built on the hill at Montmartre. Along the Tuileries Gardens, he had the rue de Rivoli laid out, ''straight as a yew tree.'' On the site of the Bastille, he ordered that a monumental fountain be built in the shape of an elephant. Often such grandiose projects were scarcely begun. The incessant warfare and brevity of the imperial monarchy hindered construction and prevented their completion.

The Napoleonic regime, born of victory, could, in fact, only be maintained by new victories. The logic of war led to the inevitability of war. Aware of what had made him, Napoleon was quoted as telling Metternich, the Austrian Chancellor and Minister of Foreign Affairs, ''Your sovereigns, born on the throne, can let themselves be beaten twenty times and still go home to their capitals. My situation is different, because I am an upstart soldier. My domination will not survive me, from the moment I have ceased to be strong and, consequently, to be feared.''

THE EMPEROR AT WAR
1805 - 1814

The violation of the Treaty of Amiens in October 1803 meant renewed warfare with England, giving Napoleon another chance to defeat ''perfidious Albion'' (Britain). Planning to land on British soil, he concentrated his troops in the north of France, near Calais. The rout of the French fleet at Trafalgar, off Cadix, by Admiral Horatio Nelson on October 21, 1805, however, showed Napoleon that there was no way he could ever win a sea war against England. He had no choice but to acknowledge his rival's absolute dominance at sea.

On the continent, a third anti-French coalition was formed during the summer of 1805. Russia, Austria, Sweden, and Naples stood with England against France. Napoleon sent his troops to fight the Austrian army, which had invaded Bavaria. Ulm surrendered in October. On December 2, 1805, he won a decisive victory over the Austro-Russian forces at Austerlitz. The Treaty of Pressburg deprived Austria of its German and Italian possessions, which it was forced to hand over to Bavaria and France. In 1806, Prussia, worried about the Emperor's success in Germany, organized another coalition which obliged Napoleon to take up arms once again. On October 14, he crushed the two Prussian armies on the battlefields of Jena and Auerstadt. Prussia caved in. Defeated at Eylau in February 1807, then at Friedland in June, Czar Alexander I also agreed to a cease-fire. He met Napoleon

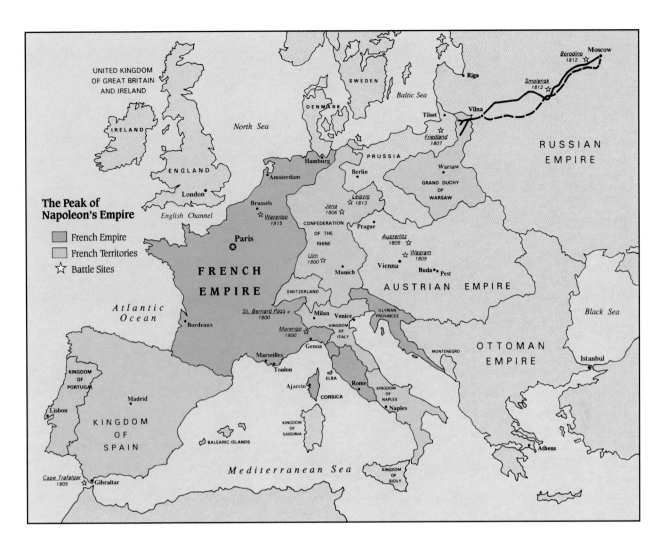

The Peak of
Napoleon's Empire

- French Empire
- French Territories
- ☆ Battle Sites

at Tilsit and suggested they become allies and divide Europe up into an Eastern Empire and a Western Empire.

Napoleon became master of Europe. The Revolution had consolidated its conquests into a Great Nation. Napoleon assembled his successes into a family network, the Great Empire. Former sister-republics became federated kingdoms under Bonaparte rule. On the throne of the Kingdom of Naples, his brother Joseph replaced the Bourbons. Louis became ruler of the former Batavian Republic, which became the Kingdom of Holland. Napoleon transformed the states along the Rhine into the Duchy of Berg, which he gave to his brother-in-law Joachim Murat. From Prussia, which lost half of its territory, he took its western provinces to create the Kingdom of Westphalia for Jerome and its eastern ones to make the Grandduchy of Warsaw. His allies, the Dukes of Bavaria and Württemberg, were made kings.

In November 1806, Napoleon consolidated his position on the continent by decreeing a blockade against England. Unable to defeat England on the battlefield or at sea, Napoleon thought to bring his enemy to its knees by asphyxiating the country economically. To be truly effective, the continental blockade had to be total. Its strict application inevitably led Napoleon on to new conquests. In 1807, he ordered his troops to occupy the ports of Hamburg, Bremen and Lübeck on the Baltic Sea. Portugal was next, although trade with England was about its only source of income. Napoleon annexed Holland and deposed Louis, whom he considered too lenient in his attempts to eliminate contraband. In 1808, the Emperor invaded Spain, which he gave to Joseph to rule. In spite of his efforts,

Napoleon's older brother never really overcame the fierce resistance of the Spaniards, who were actively supported by England. The war immobilized 300,000 of his best soldiers until 1814 without achieving notable results, when he sorely needed them on other fronts. Austria took advantage of the Emperor's difficulties in Spain to reopen hostilities in April 1809. Having won the Battle of Wagram in July, Napoleon forced Vienna to make new, major territorial concessions. He confiscated the ports of Trieste and Fiume which he made part of the Illyrian Provinces.

Napoleon also thought about the future and the dynasty he wanted to found. Yet, the Empress was unable to give him the heir he so ardently desired. In December 1809, Josephine agreed to a divorce, accepting the inevitable, while being generously compensated for her sacrifice. Napoleon immediately began looking for a new spouse. The Austrian Emperor, who was forced to recognize his adversary's military superiority, at least for the time being, let Napoleon know that he would be willing to grant him the hand of his eighteen-

Though the grandeur of his palaces may have been missing in the field of battle, Napoleon's campaign furniture reflected simplicity and elegance (see also pages 146-7).

year-old daughter, Archduchess Marie-Louise. Flattered by this offer of an alliance with the Hapsburgs, Napoleon submitted a formal request. The marriage took place by proxy in Vienna on March 10, 1810. On March 22, the new Empress arrived in France amid great pomp and circumstance. The Emperor felt like a young man again and had no doubt that he would soon have a son. The King of Rome was born on March 20, 1811. Napoleon was as deliriously happy as he was supremely powerful.

In spite of appearances, Napoleon's hold on Europe was not all that firm. Two years and three military campaigns would be enough to wrest the continent from him. The Continental Blockade did not bring England to its knees, but it did cause a serious economic crisis within the Empire. Moreover, French domination throughout Europe gave rise to nationalist sentiments among the vassal populations, which manifested more and more resistance to the French occupation of their countries. Finally, Austria and Prussia were not true allies; they were just waiting for the right moment to wreak vengeance on the French. Yet, it was Czar Alexander, unhappy about the creation of the Grandduchy of Warsaw, who was the first to betray Napoleon.

When the Emperor declared war on Russia in June 1812, the curtain rose on the final act of the imperial saga. To fight the Czar's 300,000 regular troops, Napoleon assembled an army of 600,000 men. The implacable logic of the Napoleonic system prevailed, and each vassal state furnished its contingent of soldiers. The Russians adopted a tactic known as the scorched-earth retreat, withdrawing as the enemy advanced, leaving only smoldering farms and towns in their wake, both to avoid combat and to draw the French as far as possible into their country. On September 7, Napoleon crossed the Moscow River; on the fourteenth, he entered Moscow as it burned. In a letter to Marie-Louise, dated September 18, the Emperor wrote, ''I had no idea what this city was like. There were 500 palaces as beautiful as the Elysée-Napoleon, magnificently furnished in the French style, several imperial palaces, caserns, and wonderful hospitals. Everything is gone, destroyed by the fire which has been raging for four days...It was the Governor and the Russians who, furious they had been defeated, set this beautiful city on fire...The miserable creatures even took the precaution of removing or destroying the pumps.'' On October 19, when he realized that Alexander would not sue for peace, Napoleon ordered his men to retreat. Tortured by hunger and ravaged by the cold Moscow winter, the Great Army disintegrated into a bedraggled mob, sniped at by Cossack sharpshooters. On November 29, what was left of the army escaped from their Russian pursuers and managed to cross the Berezina River. The Emperor returned to Paris, where he arrived late on the night on December 18. Behind him, he left 380,000 of his soldiers dead, wounded or prisoners of war. It was the culminating disaster. The Great Army was no more.

Napoleon at the Battle of Leipzig
(cat. No. 197, p. 163).

On February 28, 1813, Frederick-William III of Prussia abandoned the Emperor and concluded an alliance with Alexander I to wrest his country from the grip of Napoleon. On June 27, Austria defected and joined the newly formed coalition. Napoleon, however, succeeded in assembling a new army of 300,000 men, for the most part recent recruits 18 or 19 years old. One catastrophe led to another. On October 19, Napoleon had to abandon Leipzig and retreat from Germany. The Campaign of 1813 was a complete failure—all the possessions conquered by the Emperor beyond the Rhine were irreparably lost. The Austrians invaded Italy. Murat, King of Naples since 1808, and the King of Bavaria both betrayed the Emperor. The Illyrian Provinces fell at the end of October. The Tyrol revolted, and the enemy armies crossed the Alps and the Rhine (December 1813-January 1814).

For the first time in ten years, battles would no longer be fought in the far-flung reaches of the Empire but rather on home ground. Bernadotte, a French marshal and the hereditary Prince of Sweden since 1810, marched on Belgium and Holland. Blücher and Schwarzenberg advanced on Paris. With his 80,000 recruits, Napoleon attempted to stand up to the 250,000 troops the allies had massed against him, but his marshals seemed weary of war and fought only half-heartedly. The French hoped for peace. The few victories won in February were not enough to stop the allies. They continued to move toward the capital, which the Empress Marie-Louise and the government abandoned on March 28. On March 31, the coalition armies entered Paris, bringing with them the brother of Louis XVI, Louis XVIII, whom they put on the throne. On April 3, 1814, the Senate proclaimed the fall of Napoleon. The Emperor, who had taken refuge at Fontainebleau, abdicated on April 6. The allies allowed him to keep his title of Emperor and granted him sovereignty over the island of Elba, located in the Mediterranean between Corsica and Tuscany. By the Treaty of Paris, signed on May 30, 1814, France was forced to surrender the territories it had acquired during the Revolution, and the borders of 1792 were re-established.

ELBA AND SAINT HELENA
1814 - 1821

On April 20, 1814, Napoleon bade farewell to his faithful followers in the courtyard of the Château of Fontainebleau. He left France for Elba, his tiny principality which measured only 85.7 square miles and had only 12,000 inhabitants. On May 4, the Emperor landed at Portoferraio, the capital of his new realm. One can wonder how someone who wanted to be emperor of the world could be satisfied with ruling over a miniature kingdom. Yet not

easily discouraged, Napoleon took his role as sovereign very seriously. He ordered the olive groves to be replanted, built roads and hospitals, and made sure drinking water was readily available to the population. At the Mulini Palace, his official residence, he recreated a sort of imperial court with a formal etiquette. Pauline, the lovely Princess Borghese, and his mother, known as *Madame Mère*, arrived to share his exile, but the Empress Marie-Louise refused. Balls and stage-plays kept them all from being bored.

Courtyard of the
Château of Fontainebleau.

40

In spite of close surveillance by the Austrians and the French, Napoleon received thousands of letters from all over Europe. Numerous visitors brought him the latest newspapers from London and Paris. From them, he learned of the death of the Empress Josephine, who died at Malmaison on May 29 from complications brought on by a very bad cold and by anxiety about the Emperor.

Napoleon kept abreast of developments in France, where popular discontent was on the rise. Citizens feared that Louis XVIII, who had no great support among the people, would try to re-establish the *Ancien Régime*. With the return of the monarchy, the freedoms and advantages won by the Revolution would disappear. Napoleon also knew that his partisans were numerous and well-organized. A Bonapartist party had been formed around Maret, the Emperor's former Secretary of State. The army had rallied around the king with little enthusiasm, and the young generals looked to the Emperor for leadership. Napoleon decided to leave his home of exile. Why not tempt fate again?

He embarked from Elba on February 26, 1815, at nightfall, and having succeeded in avoiding the English frigates, landed on French soil in the Golfe Juan near Antibes on March 1. Spontaneously, even miraculously, from Grenoble to Lyon, he was acclaimed, and the troops rallied to him. Maréchal Ney, sent to arrest him, threw himself at the Emperor's feet. The Eagle soared. On March 20, Napoleon arrived in Paris. To cries of "Long live the Emperor," he returned to the Tuileries Palace, which Louis XVIII had just fled to take refuge in Ghent, Belgium. The vast majority of the peasants and workers supported him adamantly, while the professional classes, the bourgeois and the aristocrats hesitated, when they were not outright hostile. Napoleon knew it was risky to rely only on the popular classes. He tried to appease the elite and to fulfill their democratic expectations by establishing a liberal constitution in his Additional Act to the Constitutions of the Empire. Many observers felt, however, that Napoleon was not a sincere supporter of parliamentary monarchy and that the act was just a political maneuver. The treacherous Fouché, Minister of the Police, predicted that "things would be settled in four months." It appeared obvious that the adventure could not possibly succeed. In fact, Napoleon's return to power lasted only 100 days. From the start, Napoleon's political survival was compromised by the betrayal of the marshals, who were anxious for peace in

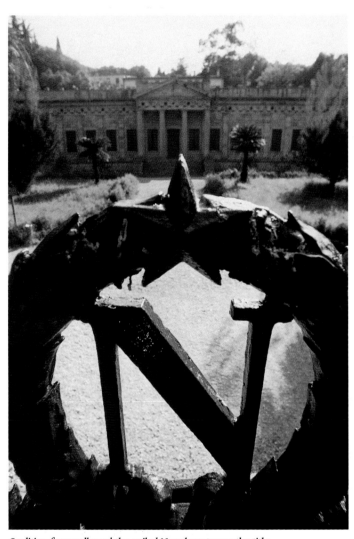

Coalition forces allowed the exiled Napoleon to use the title Emperor of the Isle of Elba. While on the island, Napoleon chose the villa of San Martino (above) as one of his residences. There, he reorganized Elba's government, drilled troops, entertained visitors, and plotted his return to France.

Napoleon found life on St. Helena to be a stark contrast
to what he had experienced on Elba.

order to benefit from the wealth they had accumulated, the passivity of the government,
the hesitancy of the bourgeoisie, and royalist resistance in western France. Above all, his
fate depended on the reaction of the allied sovereigns who were meeting at the Congress of

St. Helena - Napoleon's Final Exile
1815 - 1821

Vienna. As soon as they received word of the Emperor's
escape, the coalition again closed ranks against him. On
March 13, the allies declared him an outlaw and refused
to negotiate.

Since he had no choice but to fight, Napoleon decided
to take the offensive. On June 13, he entered Belgium with
the wild hope that he could eliminate the Anglo-Prussian
armies of Wellington and Blücher before their reinforcements
arrived. On June 16, at Ligny, he pushed back the Prussians
without, however, really defeating them. He then turned
on the English who were solidly entrenched near the
village of Waterloo (approximately six miles south of
Brussels). The battle, which began on June 18, was one
of the fiercest the imperial army had ever fought. Yet the
French efforts were in vain, and the allies were victorious.

Defeated, Napoleon returned to Paris. He still thought
he could count on the support of the nation, but the
deputies in the National Assembly demanded that he
resign. On June 22, in the Elysée Palace, he abdicated in
favor of the King of Rome. "My political life is finished,"
he wrote, "and I proclaim my son, under the title
Napoleon II, Emperor of the French... Unite for the good

of the nation and remain independent." Even this solution proved unsatisfactory, as there was general opposition to a Napoleonic dynasty. Even the return of Louis XVIII seemed the lesser of the two evils.

Completely abandoned, an outlaw in his own country, Napoleon had no choice but flight or surrender. After stopping at the Château of Malmaison in memory of Josephine, the deposed Emperor went to Rochefort on the western coast of France. On July 9, he took up residence on the island of Aix, but for the first time in his life, the future looked bleak. Should he go to America? In that land of opportunity, he could begin a new life. To do so, he would have to fight his way past the English squadron patrolling the coast, and Napoleon had lost any desire to fight. The best thing was to surrender to the English.

Napoleon Dictating His Memoirs to General Gourgaud (cat. no. 206, p. 170).

"I have come, like Themistocles, to claim hospitality at the hearth of the British people," he wrote to the Prince Regent of England. "I place myself under the protection of their laws." On July 15, he boarded the British man-of-war *Bellerophon* which took him to Plymouth. On July 31, the Emperor learned he would be deported to Saint Helena, a tiny volcanic island in the middle of the south Atlantic with its nearest neighbor 800 miles away.

In a certain way, the saga ends here, for the six years of exile Napoleon spent on Saint Helena seemed more like a period of suspended animation than another chapter in the adventure-filled life of the Emperor. Reminiscing at length and expounding on his fate, Napoleon himself forged the raw material of the legend that was to succeed him. When he died on May 5, 1821, his death was not a major event, for the Emperor had already entered the world of myths in which the hero survives, never to be forgotten, crowned with immortality.

The solitude of Napoleon's exile and tomb has bestowed on a glorious memory another sort of prestige...He sleeps like a hermit or like a pariah in a valley, at the end of a deserted path. The greatness of the silence which envelops him is equal to the immensity of the clamor which surrounded him...Where does he lie today? He lies amid ashes whose weight tipped the balance of the globe.

René de Chateaubriand, *Mémoires d'outre-tombe, 1849*

Catalogue
of the
Exhibition

PORTRAIT GALLERY

Carrara, which for centuries had produced some of Italy's finest marble, became part of Elisa Bonaparte's domain in 1806. Napoleon's sister had Italian sculptors make marble busts of the members of her family, particularly the Emperor. Under the direction of Lorenzo Bartolini (1777-1850), they carved busts in Carrara marble after plaster originals by well-known artists of the period such as Chinard, Chaudet, Bosio, and Canova.

1 Colossal Bust of Napoleon As First Consul

After Antonio Canova (1757-1822)
Marble
H: 71 x L: 50.8 cm. (28 x 20")
Roger Prigent, New York

In 1802-1803, Canova carved a colossal bust of the First Consul which he used for the head of his monumental statue of Napoleon as Mars the Pacificator. He completed the statue in 1806, and today it may be seen in the Wellington Museum, Apsley House, London. The Olympian majesty of the statue's head provoked such admiration that numerous copies were made by Canova himself, by his students and by the Carrara sculptors. The work's majestic beauty and expressive physiognomy make this imperial mask the equal of the most beautiful classical busts.

2 Bust of *Madame Mère*, née Letizia Ramolino, Napoleon's Mother

Carrara workshop, after Canova (1757-1822)
Marble
H: 58 cm. (22⅞")
Musée National du Château de Malmaison, MM 40-47-6837
Gift of Count Joseph Primoli (great-grandson of Lucien and Joseph Bonaparte)

The original work by Canova was exhibited in the Salon of 1808 and is now in the collection of the Duke of Devonshire at Chatsworth.

Letizia Ramolino was born in Ajaccio in 1749, the daughter of a noble family originally from Tuscany. In 1764, at the age of 15, she married Charles-Marie Bonaparte, a young eighteen-year-old lawyer, by whom she had thirteen children, eight of which survived. The success of her son Napoleon did not impress her, and she did not attend the Coronation in 1804, preferring to remain in Rome with her son Lucien. When she returned to Paris, she held a very high rank at Court, and after 1805, her official title was ''Her Imperial Highness, *Madame Mère*, the Mother of the Emperor.'' When Napoleon was overthrown and exiled, she followed him to Elba, but was not able to go to Saint Helena. She then returned to Rome where, crippled and blind, she outlived her son, dying there in 1836.

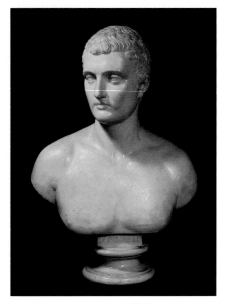

3 Bust of Charles-Marie Bonaparte, Napoleon's Father

Carrara workshop, after Joseph-Charles Marin (1759-1834)
Marble
H: 70 cm. (27½")
Fondation Dosne-Thiers, Musée Frédéric Masson, Paris
Signed BARTOLINI, after the original work which Marin completed after the death of Napoleon's father.

Charles-Marie Bonaparte was born in Ajaccio in 1746, the son of a family which came to Corsica from Genoa in the fifteenth century. Having obtained his law degree, he was named assessor of the royal jurisdiction of Ajaccio. He strove unstintingly to be recognized as a noble so that he could send his children to the schools of the King of France. He died in 1785 in Montpellier, where he had gone for treatment of a malignant tumor.

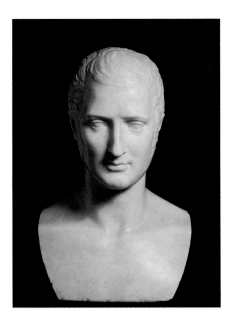

4 Bust of Joseph Bonaparte

Carrara workshop, most probably after François-Nicolas Delaistre (1746-1832)
Marble
H: 48 cm. (19″)
Musée National de la Maison Bonaparte, Ajaccio, Corsica, N 38
Gift of Prince and Princess Napoleon in 1979

The bust belonged to Princess de la Moskowa, who died in 1949 and who was a descendent
of both Lucien and Joseph Bonaparte.

Joseph Bonaparte, the eldest son of Charles and Letizia, was born in Corte in 1768.
In 1794, he married Julie Clary, the daughter of a rich Marseille trader. He participated
in his younger brother's rise to power, going on various diplomatic missions and nego-
tiating with Austria, England and the United States (the Treaty of Mortefontaine). He
became a Senator and then a Grand-Officier of the Legion of Honor. In 1806, the
Emperor gave him the Kingdom of Naples, which he traded for the Spanish throne in
1808. After French defeats, he was forced to leave Madrid. In 1814 the Emperor made
him a lieutenant-general with orders to defend Paris. Nonetheless, Joseph had to abandon
the capital, and he retreated to Switzerland. During the Hundred Days, he presided over
the Council of Ministers in the Emperor's absence. After Waterloo, he fled to the United
States and settled in Point Breeze near Philadelphia. He died in Florence in 1844.

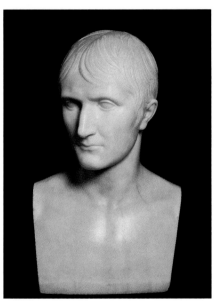

5 Bust of Lucien Bonaparte

Carrara workshop, possibly after Antonio Canova (1757-1822)
Marble
H: 48 cm. (19″)
Musée National de la Maison Bonaparte, Ajaccio, Corsica, N 39
Gift of Prince and Princess Napoleon
This bust also once belonged to Princess de la Moskowa.

Lucien, the Bonapartes' third child, was born in Ajaccio in 1775. Although he had actively
supported the Jacobin cause during the French Revolution, he became more moderate
and was named President of the Council of the Five Hundred in 1799. After having
played an important role in the coup of 18 *Brumaire* which enabled Napoleon to take
power, he became Minister of the Interior and then Ambassador to Madrid. Shortly after
the death of his first wife, Lucien decided to remarry and chose Alexandrine Jacob de
Bleschamp, just when Napoleon was planning to have him marry the Queen of Etruria.
The relationship between the two brothers deteriorated rapidly and then was broken off
completely. Lucien took refuge in Rome, in the Papal States. In 1810, on his way from
Rome to seek asylum in the United States, he was captured by the English and kept
prisoner in Great Britain for three years. It was only in 1815 that the two brothers resolved
their differences, and Lucien was named a French prince. He spent the rest of his life
in Italy and died in Viterbo in 1840.

6 Bust of Elisa Bonaparte

Carrara workshop, after Lorenzo Bartolini (1777-1850)
Marble
H: 68 cm. (26¾″)
Musée National du Château de Malmaison, MM 40-47-814
On loan from the Musée National du Château de Versailles since 1907

The eldest Bonaparte daughter was born in Ajaccio in 1777 and, as a young lady from
a noble family, was admitted to the prestigious Saint-Cyr School. In 1797, when she was
twenty, she married a rather ordinary Corsican officer, Felix Bacciochi. Very rapidly, she
learned that her devouring ambition could help compensate for her ungracious physical
appearance. She succeeded in having her brother name her Princess of Piombino in
1805, and of Lucca in 1806, and finally Grand Duchess of Tuscany in 1809. She took
her role as ruler very seriously, and proved to be both an active patron of the arts and
a competent overseer of her estates. After the fall of the Empire, she went to live in Italy,
where she died in 1820.

7 Bust of Louis Bonaparte

Carrara workshop, after Pierre Cartellier (1757-1831)
Marble
H: 54 cm. (21¼")
Bibliothèque Marmottan, Boulogne-Billancourt, Inv. 70-332

The bust comes from one of the palaces of King Jerome Bonaparte near Cassel, Germany.

Louis Bonaparte was born in Ajaccio in 1778 and raised by his brother Napoleon. He became Napoleon's aide-de-camp during the Italian and Egyptian campaigns. Josephine, who wanted to link the fortunes of the Beauharnais and the Bonaparte families more closely, had him marry her daughter, Hortense, in 1802. Both of the spouses were unhappy, however, and finally separated. First named Grand Constable, Louis was made King of Holland in 1806, but ignoring his brother's injunctions, he supported Dutch interests instead of giving his full support to the French blockade against England. In 1810, he was forced to flee to Austria, and Holland became part of the French Empire. Retiring from politics, he turned to literature and lived in Italy until the fall of the Empire. He died in Livorno in 1846.

8 Bust of Pauline Bonaparte

Carrara workshop, after Antonio Canova (1757-1822)
Marble
H: 45 cm. (17¾")
Musée National du Château de Malmaison, MM 40-47-6835

The original of this bust is now in the Borghese Gallery in Rome. It comes from the collection of the Empress Eugénie and was a gift of Count Joseph Primoli (great-grandson of Lucien and Joseph Bonaparte).

Pauline was born in Ajaccio in 1780. In 1797, when she was just seventeen, Napoleon decided to marry his sister to Victor-Emmanuel Leclerc, a valorous soldier, who unfortunately died of yellow fever in 1802 during the aborted expedition to Santo-Domingo. The following year, concerned about the young widow's reputation, Napoleon hurriedly had her marry Prince Camille Borghese, the heir to a noble Roman family. In 1806, although separated from her husband, she became Princess Borghese and Duchess of Guastalla, leading a life of luxury, full of romantic intrigues. Always devoted and faithful to her older brother, she went to Elba in 1814 to be with Napoleon and unsuccessfully tried to reach Saint Helena. She returned to Italy and died in Florence in 1825.

9 Bust of Caroline Bonaparte

Carrara workshop, after the original by Antonio Canova (1757-1822)
Marble
H: 70 cm. (27½")
Musée Marmottan, Paris, Inv. 946
Gift of Paul Marmottan

Napoleon's youngest sister was born in Ajaccio in 1782. After receiving a proper education at the academy of Madame Campan, she married Joachim Murat, a handsome horseman who was one of Napoleon's faithful followers, in 1800. She was not satisfied with the title of Imperial Highness that the Emperor had bestowed on her. She wanted a kingdom as well, but her ambition had to settle for the Grand Duchy of Berg and Cleves, which was given to the Murats in 1806. Only in 1808 did they receive the Kingdom of Naples. There, they tried to exercise a certain degree of independence, something which the Emperor was by no means prepared to grant. Their betrayal of Napoleon in 1814 cost them their throne. After the execution of her husband in 1815, Caroline lived in Italy under the pseudonym of Countess de Lipona (an anagram of Napoli, the Italian name for Naples). She died in Florence in 1839.

10 Bust of Jerome Bonaparte

Carrara workshop, after François-Joseph Bosio (1768-1845)
Marble
H: 54 cm. (21¼")
Bibliothèque Marmottan, Boulogne-Billancourt, Inv.70-123
Gift of Paul Marmottan

Jerome, the Bonapartes' youngest child, was born in Ajaccio in 1784. Lacking serious motivation, he was sent by his brother to sail the Mediterranean and the Atlantic. During a stopover in Baltimore in 1803, he married the young American Elizabeth Patterson without his family's consent. Soon after returning to Europe with his pregnant wife, Napoleon convinced him to have the marriage annulled, and Jerome became a French prince. In 1807, he married Princess Catherine, the daughter of the new King of Württemberg, and that same year was named King of Westphalia. The couple took up residence in Cassel, where Jerome thought more about leading a life of leisure than about salvaging his kingdom, which was made up of disparate territories. They had to relinquish their thrones in 1813 and take refuge in France. After Waterloo, where he fought courageously, Jerome was exiled first to Austria, then to Rome. When his nephew Louis-Napoleon took power, he returned to politics. He was named Governor of the Invalides, Maréchal of France and President of the Senate. Jerome died in 1860 in the Château of Villegenis, the house he owned near Paris.

11 Bust of Josephine

Carrara workshop, after Antoine-Denis Chaudet (1763-1810)
Marble
H: 50 cm. (19¾")
Musée National du Château de Malmaison, MM 40-47-6831

The inscription BARTOLINI DIR. on the bust indicates that it was carved by one of the Carrara sculptors under the direction of Lorenzo Bartolini (1777-1850), after the original by Antoine-Denis Chaudet.

12 Bust of Marie-Louise

Lorenzo Bartolini (1777-1850), after
   François-Joseph Bosio (1768-1845)
Marble
H: 71 cm. (28")
Musée Marmottan, Paris, Inv. 948

The bust bears the inscription BARTOLINI DIREXIT DE BOSIO, which proves that it came from Carrara. François-Joseph Bosio sculpted the original work in 1810 at the Compiègne Palace, realistically portraying the new Empress' round eyes and Hapsburg lip.

13 Bust of Felix Bacciochi, Husband of Elisa Bonaparte

Carrara workshop, after Lorenzo Bartolini (1777-1850)
Marble
H: 57 cm. (22⅜")
Bibliothèque Marmottan, Boulogne-Billancourt, Inv. 70-330
Gift of Paul Marmottan

Felix Bacciochi was born in Ajaccio in 1762, the son of a noble Genoese family which had settled in Corsica. An undistinguished soldier, he married Napoleon's sister, Elisa Bonaparte, in 1797 and profited from Napoleon's rise to power. First Prince of Piombino, then of Lucca, he remained in the background when his wife became Grand Duchess of Tuscany in 1809, apparently satisfied with being a cuckolded Prince Consort without any real power. After the fall of the Empire, he went to live in Italy. He died in Bologna in 1841.

14 Bust of Joachim Murat

Carrara workshop, perhaps after Antonio Canova (1757-1822)
Marble
H: 69 cm. (27¼")
Musée Marmottan, Paris, Inv. 938

Son of an innkeeper, Joachim Murat was born in La Bastide-Fortunière in southwestern France in 1767. Destined for a military career, he rose rapidly through the ranks during the Revolution and helped Napoleon squash the insurrection of 13 *Vendémiaire* (October 5, 1795). The fate of the two men was then linked. This bond was strengthened by Murat's marriage to Caroline Bonaparte in 1800. Maréchal of the Empire, Prince and Grand Admiral in 1805, his cavalry played an important role in numerous French victories. First named Grand Duke of Berg and Cleves in 1806, he became King of Naples in 1808 and was considered a good ruler. Worried that the fall of Napoleon might mean the loss of his kingdom, Murat signed a treaty with Austria, which enabled him to remain on the throne, at least for the time being. In 1815, when Napoleon returned from Elba, Murat rallied to his cause, but the Emperor eschewed his help. When Murat tried to reconquer his kingdom, he was arrested and shot in Pizzo in 1815 by order of the House of Bourbon.

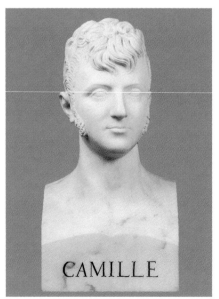

15 Bust of Camille, Prince Borghese

Carrara workshop, perhaps after Giovanni-Battista Comoli (1775-1830)
Marble
H: 56 cm. (22")
Musée National du Château de Versailles, MV 1541

Purchased by Napoleon III from the daughter of Elisa Bonaparte in 1854

Nine months after General Leclerc was killed, leaving Pauline a widow, Napoleon had her marry the Roman prince Camille Borghese (1775-1832), a handsome man of limited intelligence. Husband and wife lived very little together. In 1808, Camille Borghese was made Governor General of the Empire's cisalpine administrative departments. After the fall of the Empire, they lived separately.

16 House in Which Napoleon Was Born

Léonard-Alexis Daligé de Fontenay (1813-1892)
Oil on canvas, 1849
H: 38 x L: 46 cm. (15 x 18″)
Musée National du Château de Malmaison, MM 40-47-7218
Salon of 1849; collection of Napoleon III; gift of Laussedat, 1929

Also shown page 25

Except for Joseph, whose birthplace was Corte, Napoleon and
all his brothers and sisters were born in this house, located in
the old city of Ajaccio. It came into the family in 1682, but was
restored and refurnished after having been firebombed by the
followers of Paoli in 1793. It remained in the imperial family until
1923, when it was given to the French government by Prince-
Victor-Napoleon. It is now a national museum and has been
under the authority of the curator of the Château of Malmaison
since 1967.

17 Napoleon's Cradle

Walnut, end of the eighteenth century
H: 54 x L: 110 x W: 58 cm. (21¼ x 43¼ x 22 ⁷/₈″)
Private collection, Ajaccio, Corsica

Letizia Bonaparte used this cradle for all her children until 1779,
when she gave it to her husband's cousin who had just given
birth to her first child. Since then, the cradle has remained in
that family.

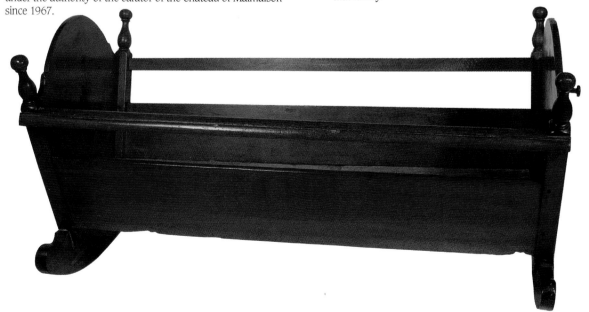

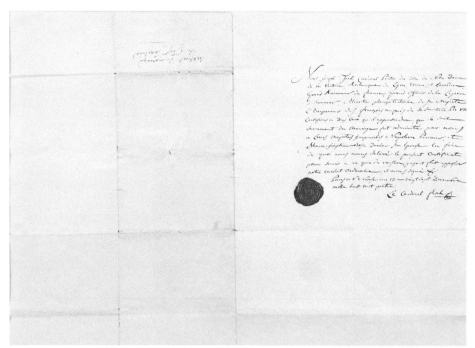

18 Wedding Certificate of Napoleon and Josephine

Paper, wax
H: 53 x W: 39 cm. (22⅝ x 16⅝″)
The Forbes Magazine Collection, New York

Josephine and Napoleon met in the fall of 1795 and married in a civil ceremony in Paris on March 9, 1796. Josephine was not happy with just a civil ceremony, since it was too easy to divorce in such cases. On the eve of the Coronation, she informed the Pope of their marital situation, which was not in keeping with Church teachings. Pius VII demanded that they be married in a religious ceremony, and a church wedding was celebrated on December 1, 1804, by Cardinal Fesch.

19 Wedding Basket Given by Napoleon to Josephine

Silk, silver, copper, papier maché, 1796
H: 44 x L: 54 x W: 30 cm. (17⅜ x 21¼ x 11¾″)
Musée National du Château de Malmaison, N 393
Gift of Prince and Princess Napoleon, 1979

In the eighteenth century, a husband traditionally gave his young bride a wedding basket, called a sultan, which was usually filled with jewels and trinkets. Napoleon presented this basket to Josephine when they were married in 1796.

20 **General Napoleon Bonaparte at the Bridge of Arcole**

Antoine-Jean, baron Gros (1773-1835)
Oil on canvas, 1796
H: 130 x L: 94 cm. (51⅛ x 37″)
Musée National du Château de Versailles, MV 6314
Salon of 1801; collection of the First Consul, then of Napoleon III; gift of Empress Eugénie, 1879

Also shown page 27

The painting captures the moment on November 17, 1796, when Bonaparte, with a flag in his hand, leads the Augereau grenadiers across the bridge over the Adige at Arcole. The young general's courage and daring are magnificently represented. By all reports, Gros' portrait was a very good likeness because Josephine kept Napoleon still by having him sit on her lap.

21

21 The Battle of Rivoli

Giuseppe Pietro Bagetti (1764-1831)
Watercolor, 1797
H: 54 x L: 82 cm. (21¼" x 32¼")
Musée National du Château de Versailles, MV 2506

Bagetti was a landscape painter hired by Bonaparte to paint the highlights of his military career. The Battle of Rivoli was fought on January 14, 1797, against the Austrians in the foothills of the Alps east of the Lago di Garda. The watercolor shows the moment when the French army attacked the enemy soldiers and made them retreat from the positions they had previously taken.

22 View of Lodi

Parent, after Giuseppe Pietro Bagetti (1764-1831)
Watercolor, 1796
H: 53 x L: 80 cm. (20⅞ x 31½")
Musée National du Château de Versailles, MV 2483

In Lodi, during the first Italian Campaign, Bonaparte personally oversaw artillery operations, determining the location of the cannons in order to set a trap for the Austrians. It was this incident that earned him the nickname "the little Corporal."

22

23 Bonaparte Visiting the Plague-Stricken Soldiers in the Hospital at Jaffa

Antoine-Jean, baron Gros (1773-1835)
Oil on canvas, circa 1804
H: 118 x L: 167 cm. (46½ x 65¾")
Museum of Fine Arts, Boston
Acquired thanks to the S. A. Denio Fund

The original, exhibited in the Salon of 1804, is in the Louvre in Paris.
   This copy, undoubtedly by the artist himself, came from the collection
   of the Duke of Trévise, a descendent of Maréchal Mortier.

When Bonaparte left Egypt on his way to Syria, he entered Jaffa after having set siege to the city and massacred 3,000 of the enemy. But the next day, the plague broke out, and between 7,000 and 8,000 of his troops died. Unmindful of the danger, Bonaparte visited a hospital on March 11, 1799. However, it is not sure he touched a soldier's open sore. Gros' interpretation was meant to impress Napoleon's soldiers and serve as propaganda.

26

24 *La Description de l'Egypte*

Paper, leather binding by Tessier 1810, 2 folio volumes
H: 69.5 x L: 54 cm. each (27³/₈ x 21¼")
Musée National du Château de Malmaison, MM 40-47-6815
  and MM 40-47-6816
Gift of Mr. and Mrs. John Jaffé, 1933

When Bonaparte was planning his Egyptian Campaign, he decided to have 36 scholars accompany him. Their job was to record all the pertinent scientific and artistic information on the country he was setting out to conquer. The Egyptian Commission coordinated operations and supervised the publication of the reports when the expedition returned. Begun in 1809, this gigantic undertaking was not finished until 1828. The work contains a total of 900 engraved plates. The Château of Malmaison has copies of the first three volumes, the only ones published during the Empire, in their original 1810 bindings with the coat of arms. The full title of the work shown is *La Description de l'Egypte ou recueil des observations et des recherches qui ont été faites en Egypte pendant l'expédition de l'Armée française, publié par les ordres de Sa Majesté Napoléon le Grand,* Paris, Imprimerie Impériale, 1809.

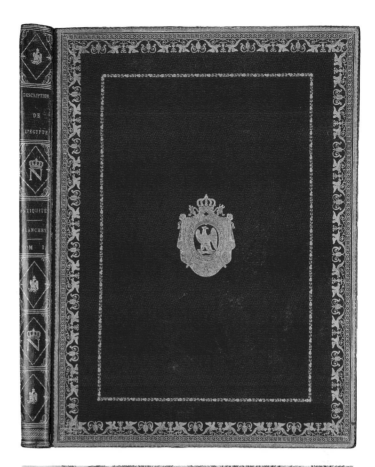

25 View of Memphis

Jean-Louis Delignon (1755-circa 1830), after André Dutertre
  (1753-1842)
Engraving, 1809
H: 70 x L: 55 cm. (27½ x 21⁵/₈")
Musée National du Château de Malmaison, MM bibliothéque
  1117 (5)

This view of the ruins of ancient Memphis is from the *Description de l'Egypte, Antiquités,* vol. V. plate 3.

26 The Battle of the Pyramids

Louis-François, baron Lejeune (1775-1848)
Oil on canvas, 1806
H: 180 x L: 425 cm. (5' 7½" x 13' 7⁷/₈")
Signed: LEJEUNE, CHEF DE BATAILLON AU CORPS
  IMPÉRIAL DU GÉNIE À PARIS, 1806
Musée National du Château de Versailles, MV 6854

Salon of 1806; purchased in 1861

The first major battle between the Mamelukes and the French Eastern Army, commanded by Bonaparte, took place on July 21, 1798. At the foot of the pyramids, the young general harangued his troops, whipping up their courage to fight for the victory which would open the doors of Cairo to the French.

27 **Portraits of Sheiks Cherkaoui and El Bekry**
28 Michele Rigo (1770-1815)
Oil on canvas, circa 1805-1810
H: 100 x L: 83 cm. (39 3/8 x 32 5/8") each
Private collection, Paris

The Italian artist Michele Rigo took part in the Egyptian expedition and painted the portraits of several sheiks of the Cairo Divan who supported Bonaparte. Since it was forbidden by the Koran to represent the human face, the sheiks were anything but reassured. Rigo completed several series of portraits, including one for Bonaparte which is in the collection of the Château of Malmaison. These two portraits possibly belonged to Maréchal Bessières. Sheik Abdullah Cherkaoui (1740-1812) presided over the Cairo Divan, and Sheik El Seyd Khalil Bekry (died 1808) was one of the council members.

29 Sash Worn by Napoleon

Wool, cashmere
L: 200 x W: 60 cm. (78¾ x 23⅝")
Musée National du Château de Malmaison, N 288
Gift of Prince Napoleon and the Countess de Witt, 1979

This red, white and blue sash was part of the uniform of
a general of the Republic. Bonaparte wore it tied around
his waist during the Egyptian Campaign. It remained
in the collection of the imperial family until 1979.

30 Saber Worn by Napoleon

Steel, ivory, copper gilt, wood, velvet
L: 82 cm. (32¼")
Musée de l'Armée, Paris (on loan from the Louvre),
  O.A. 10425

Given to the French government in payment of inheritance
  taxes, 1973

Most likely Turkish and taken from a Mameluke on the
battlefield, Bonaparte used this saber during the Battle
of the Pyramids on July 21, 1798. The Murat family
acquired the saber during the nineteenth century, and
it became one of the family's treasures, always passed
down to the eldest son.

31 Mameluke Saddle

Silk, velvet, red leather, silver gilt, end of the 18th century
H: 132 x L: 172 x W: 53 cm. (52 x 67¾ x 20⅞")
Musée de l'Armée, Paris, Cd 73

After the Battle of the Pyramids, Bonaparte's staff
officers gave him several saddles and harnesses,
including this magnificent Mameluke saddle, together
with its saddle blanket, stirrups and pistols. It has
belonged to the French government ever since.

32 Bonaparte as First Consul

Antoine-Jean, baron Gros (1773-1835)
Oil on canvas, 1802
H: 227 x L: 149 cm. (89 3/8 x 58 5/8″) in original frame
Signed and dated: GROS A PARIS AN X
Musée National de la Légion d'Honneur et des Ordres de Chevalerie,
   Paris, Inv. 04378

Presented by Bonaparte to the Second Consul, Cambacérès, as
   indicated on the (original) frame

Also shown page 29

Dressed in his red velvet suit decorated with gold embroidery
and wearing the Regent diamond sword, Bonaparte is represented
at the height of his glory as First Consul. Above the maps of
the Saint Bernard Pass and of the Marengo battlefield, Gros
inscribed the names of the treaties of Plaisance, Tolentino,
Léoben, Campo-Formio, Lunéville, and Amiens, as well as
those of 18 *Brumaire*, the Concordat and the Lyon Assembly.

33 Meeting of the Council of the Five Hundred at Saint Cloud

Jacques Sablet (1749-1803)
Oil on canvas
H: 66 x L: 84.5 cm. (26 x 33¼″)
Musée des Beaux-Arts, Nantes, MBA 811.1.2 P
Purchase 1811

Even if the ruling Directors resigned on 18 *Brumaire*, the real
coup took place the following day, 19 *Brumaire* (November 10,
1799). The Assembly of the Five Hundred met outside Paris in
the Orangery of the Château of Saint Cloud. At the meeting,
Bonaparte's presence galvanized the deputies. Without the
intervention of the Assembly president, Lucien Bonaparte, and
of the troops which cleared the hall, there would have been no
coup d'état. An eyewitness, Jacques Sablet painted this work
in two hours immediately after the session.

34 Red Suit of Bonaparte, First Consul

Velvet, silk, gold, silver
H: 113 cm. (44½″)
Musée National du Château de Malmaison, N 259
Acquired in 1979 from the collection of the imperial family

This suit was presented to the First Consul by the City of Lyon, most likely on his return from Marengo in June 1800. The Lyonnais probably wanted to impress Bonaparte with the quality goods for which the city was known. The First Consul wore the suit on several occasions, such as at the ceremony in Notre-Dame on April 18, 1802, when the *Te Deum* was sung to celebrate the Concordat, and at the signing of the Concordat itself. It should not be confused with another suit, also in red velvet, which figures in official portraits of Bonaparte by Gros, Ingres and Greuze. Napoleon took this suit with him to Saint Helena. In 1818, he gave it to the daughter of the Grand-Maréchal Bertrand, Hortense Bertrand, so that she could use the material to make a dress. Fortunately, she did not do so, and later bequeathed the suit to Prince Victor-Napoleon.

*35 **Relation de la bataille de Marengo présentée
à l'Empereur sur le champ de bataille Par le
Maréchal d'Empire Alexandre Berthier, le 24
Prairial AN 13, anniversaire de la Victoire
Napoleon at Marengo***

Carle Vernet (1758-1835)
Watercolor and gouache
H: 66 x L: 50 cm. (26 x 19 ⁵/₈ ")
Musée National du Château de Malmaison, MM 40-47-6830
Napoleon's personal copy; Marie-Louise's library in Vienna;
  gift of Mr. and Mrs. John Jaffé, 1933

This account of the battle was written by Berthier,
the Minister of War, who presented the work to the
Emperor on June 14, 1804, the anniversary of the
battle. Napoleon's personal copy has a magnificent
green leather binding by Bizouard with the Empire
coat of arms.

36 The Battle of Marengo

Parent, after Giuseppe Pietro Bagetti (1764-1831)
Watercolor
H: 53 x L: 80 cm. (20⅞ x 31½″)
Musée National du Château de Versailles, MV 2545

37 The Death of General Desaix

Morel, after Giuseppe Pietro Bagetti (1764-1831)
Watercolor
H: 54 x L: 80 cm. (21¼ x 31½″)
Musée National du Château de Versailles, MV 2546

Unable to negotiate peace with England and Austria, Bonaparte had no choice but to fight. After crossing the
Alps, he triumphantly entered Milan and re-established the Cisalpine Republic. Almost immediately, however,
he was obliged to confront the Austrian army, massed at Marengo on June 14, 1800. He had only 25,000 men
as compared with the 77,000 the Austrian general had at his disposal, and 15 cannons as compared with 100.
After almost losing the battle, the French were finally victorious. The peace which was then concluded crowned
Bonaparte's efforts, and his popularity attained new heights. France maintained control of Italy as far as the
Adige, and Austria gave up its claims. The artist chose to represent the moment of victory, achieved only after
the decisive intervention of General Desaix, who unfortunately perished during the height of the battle from
a bullet wound to his heart.

38 Napoleon Bonaparte Crossing the Alps by the Great Saint Bernard Pass

Jacques-Louis David (1748-1825)
Oil on canvas, 1800
H: 260 x L: 221 cm. (87 x 102 ⅜")
Signed and dated: L. David-L'AN IX
Musée National du Château de Malmaison, MM 49-7-1
Bequeathed to the museum in 1949 by Princess de la Moskowa, the great-granddaughter of Joseph Bonaparte, King of Spain

Also shown on cover

David and his assistants painted five versions of this famous portrait. This one was the first. King Charles IV of Spain ordered it in 1800 for the Royal Palace in Madrid, and David painted it in four months. Having become King of Spain, Joseph Bonaparte took the painting with him when he was forced to leave Madrid. The picture hung in his house in Point Breeze near Philadelphia for many years until it was returned to Europe. David chose to romanticize the event by changing the sure-footed mule on which Bonaparte crossed the Alps into a dashing charger. The hero is depicted in the uniform he wore at the Battle of Marengo. David painted the uniform accurately, because he had it brought to his studio.

39 Uniform Worn by Bonaparte

Fabric
H: 115 cm. (45¼")
Musée de l'Armée, Paris, Ca 14

Left in safekeeping by Napoleon's Chamberlin, the Count of Turenne, in 1814; given by Napoleon III to the Musée des Souverains; since then in national collections (the vest and neck-scarf are modern)

This is a typical general's uniform of the period, as described in the instructions of August 7, 1798. Bonaparte wore this uniform at the Battle of Marengo, and it is the uniform he is shown wearing in David's picture *Napoleon Crossing the Alps by the Great Saint Bernard Pass.*

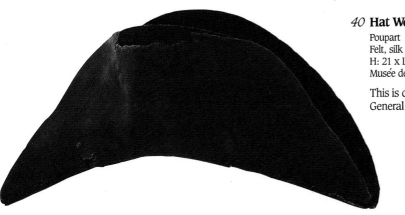

40 Hat Worn by Bonaparte

Poupart
Felt, silk
H: 21 x L: 42 x W: 21 cm. (8¼ x 16½ x 8¼")
Musée de l'Armée, Paris, Ca 8

This is one of the oldest hats known to have belonged to General Bonaparte. He wore it at the Battle of Marengo.

41 Congress of Amiens

Anatole Devosge (1770-1850)
Oil on canvas
H: 100 x L: 130 cm. (39³/₈ x 51⅛")
Fondation Dosne-Thiers, Musée Frédéric Masson, Inv. 2029

After the signing of the Treaty of Lunéville on February 9, 1801, England stood alone against France. Once Pitt left the government, a peace treaty was signed in Amiens by Joseph Bonaparte and Lord Cornwallis on March 25, 1802. The respite granted to the Consulate and the Empire lasted only one year; hostilities erupted again in March 1803. This allegory shows the First Consul signing the peace treaty, represented as a young woman, while Bellona, the Roman goddess of war, throws down her shield and takes flight.

42 Napoleonic Code

Paper, black velvet binding, quarto volume
H: 27 x W: 21 x D: 8.5 cm. (10½ x 8¼ x 3⅜″)
Bibliothèque Nationale, Paris, Rés Vélins 994

Under the *Ancien Régime*, there were several very different legal codes which royal decrees had already
tried to harmonize. Since the Revolution did not succeed in drawing up a common legislative code,
Bonaparte decided on August 12, 1800, to name a commission of four members to propose a new
code. A first project, drawn up in four months, led to a legislative phase which culminated on March 21,
1804, in the promulgation of the "Civil Code of the French," called the Napoleonic Code after 1807.
The clarity and flexibility of the new code made it a model for many other countries, and despite
a number of changes, it is still in effect in France.

43 Legion of Honor of Maréchal Berthier

Martin-Guillaume Biennais (1764-1843)
Gold, enamel
H: 40 x D: 51 cm. (15¾ x 20″) without cross
Musée National de la Légion d'Honneur et des Ordres de Chevalerie, Paris, Inv. 08161

It was in the Council Chamber of Malmaison that, in April 1802, Bonaparte suggested creating an ''honor to recognize military bravery and civilian merit.'' The law enacted on May 19, 1802, established the Legion of Honor as France's most prestigious national order, which it still is today. This decoration, designed by jeweler Martin-Guillaume Biennais, is identical to the Emperor's. It belonged to Louis-Alexandre Berthier (1753-1815), Prince of Neufchâtel and Wagram, Maréchal of France. Grand-Officier of the Legion of Honor, Berthier was named Commander of the First Cohort (the French army was then divided up into 15 cohorts).

COUNCIL CHAMBER OF MALMAISON

Bonaparte stayed at Malmaison frequently, and it soon became obvious he needed a room where he could hold cabinet meetings. Built in ten days by the French architects Percier and Fontaine, it was designed in the form of a tent supported by spears. The doors represent trophies of weapons of ancient warrior peoples, after sketches by Percier.

Many important decisions were made in the Council Chamber of Malmaison in 1801 and 1802. In addition to the ratification of the Treaty of San Ildefonso by which the Louisiana Territory was returned to France, the Act of Malmaison (a draft of a federal constitution for Switzerland) was drawn up, the Legion of Honor was created, and the sad fate of the Duke of Enghien was decided.

The only known inventory of the furniture in this room was drafted in 1814—almost fifteen years after the historic events mentioned above. Obviously, after their divorce, Josephine made some changes; consequently, it is not known what the original furnishings were. The furniture in the room, which is usually on display in the Council Chamber of Malmaison, has been restored for this exhibit thanks to the generosity of the City of Memphis.

Individual photographs of exhibited objects from the Council Chamber of Malmaison were not possible as they were under going restoration at the time of this publication.

44 Four Armchairs

Jacob-Frères (name used between 1796 and 1803 by the two Jacob brothers, Georges II and François-Honoré-Georges)
Gilt wood, red cloth, gold brocade
H: 95 x L: 52 x W: 46 cm. (37½ x 20½ x 18″)
Musée National du Château de Malmaison, MM 40-47-713 to 716
Delivered in 1802 for the Grand Salon des Consuls in the Palace of Saint Cloud; placed by Napoleon III in the Council Chamber of Malmaison; collection of the Mobilier National

45 Six Chairs

Jacob-Frères
Gilt wood, red cloth, gold brocade
H: 61 x L: 38 x W: 40 cm. (24 x 15 x 15¾″)
Musée National du Château de Malmaison, MM 40-47-717 to 722
Delivered in 1802 for the Palace of Saint Cloud; placed by Napoleon III in the Council Chamber of Malmaison; collection of the Mobilier National

46 Five Stools

Jacob-Frères
Gilt wood, red cloth, gold brocade
H: 72 x L: 75 x W: 47 cm. (28³/₈ x 29½ x 18½″)
Musée National du Château de Malmaison, MM 40-47-6961 and 6962; MM 54-9-1; MM 90-15-1 and 2
The inventory of 1814 mentions ten stools of this type in the Council Chamber. Five have now been repurchased - three came from the Council Chamber originally, and the other two were delivered for the state bedroom of Prince Murat in the Elysée Palace.

51 Three Sconces

Attributed to André-Antoine Ravrio (1759-1814)
Gilt bronze, 1805-1807
H: 75 x L: 50 cm. (29½ x 19⅝″)
Musée National du Château de Malmaison,
    MM 40-47-8374 and 8375; MMD 58-1
Not shown

Two of these sconces were put in the Council Chamber of Malmaison during the Second Empire. The third, which was in Compiègne during the Empire, was taken to Versailles during the reign of Louis-Philippe.

52 Two Andirons

François Rabiat, bronze worker
Gilt bronze, 1802
H: 49 x L: 49 x W: 16 cm. (19¼ x 19¼ x 6¼″)
Musée National du Château de Malmaison,
    MM 40-47-7222 and 7223

These andirons with military motifs came from the Hôtel de Brienne, which was the Paris residence of Napoleon's mother during the Empire.

47 Carpet

Manufacture Piat Lefebvre, Tournai
Wool
H: 6.2 x L: 5.25 m. (20′ 2⅞″ x 17′ 1⅞″)
Musée National du Château de Malmaison,
    MM 40-47-8229
Collection of the Mobilier National

Certainly delivered in 1802 by the Tournai rug weaver Piat Lefebvre and Sons for the Palace of Saint Cloud.

During the Consulate and the Empire, this carpet was in Josephine's bedroom, which became Marie-Louise's after Napoleon's remarriage.

48 Two Candelabra

Gilt bronze and marble
H: 71 x L: 42 x W: 35 cm. (28 x 16½ x 13¾″) Musée
    National du Château de Malmaison, MM 65-3-26 and 27
Gift of Baroness Gourgaud, 1965
Not shown

These magnificent Louis XVI candelabra most likely date from the beginning of the nineteenth century.

49 Table Lamp

Gilt bronze and metal
H: 73 x D: 46.5 cm. (28¾ x 18⅜″)
Musée National du Château de Malmaison,
    MM 40-47-737

Little is known of this object, except that it came to Malmaison during the reign of Napoleon III. This type of lamp was used to light desks and card tables. Its shade moved up or down to provide more or less light. It has the initials of King Louis-Philippe (LP) and is in the collection of the Mobilier National.

50 Two Candlesticks

Gilt bronze
H: 31.5 x D: 14 cm. (12⅜ x 5½″)
Musée National du Château de Malmaison,
    MM 40-47-8368 and 8369
Collection of the Mobilier National

These candlesticks decorated with female heads are a rare model bought by Napoleon III when Malmaison was redecorated during the Second Empire.

53 Table and Table Cover

Wood, velvet, silk
H: 76 x D: 180 cm. (30 x 70⅞″)
Musée National du Château de Malmaison
Table cover not shown

The table and the table cover are modern. They were modeled on the tables and covers in the Council Chambers of the Palaces of Saint Cloud and Fontainebleau.

54 Doors

Wood and material
H: 279 x L: 80 cm. (110 x 31½″)
Musée National du Château
    de Malmaison

The trophies were painted after sketches by Percier and represent the weapons of the great warrior peoples of Antiquity: the Gauls, the Daci, the Persians, and the Etruscans.

55 Eagle from Above the Doors

Painted and gilt wood
H: 39 x L: 88 cm. (15⅜ x 34⅝″)
Musée National du Château
    de Malmaison

56 Minerva Clock

Attributed to Gérard-Jean Galle
    (1788-1846)
Gilt bronze and red marble
H: 87 x L: 26.5 x W: 19.5 cm.
    (34¼ x 10½ x 7⅝″)
Musée National du Château
    de Malmaison, MM 40-47-7280
Gift of Louis S. Cates, 1939

57 Portrait of Thomas Jefferson (1743-1826)

Bouch
Pierre noire and chalk on paper, 1801
H: 53 x L: 43 cm. (20⅞ x 17″)
Musée National du Château de Malmaison, MM 58-7-2
Gift of Baroness Gourgaud, 1958

This drawing was most likely given to the First Consul by the envoys of President Jefferson when Louisiana was sold to the United States. It remained at Malmaison until the estate sale in 1829, when it was purchased by Baron Gourgaud, the Emperor's faithful companion on Saint Helena. The portrait was in the Gourgaud family collection until it was given to Malmaison in 1958.

58 Louisiana Purchase

Ink on paper, wax seals
H: 50.8 x W: 66 cm. (20 x 28¼″)
National Archives, Washington, D.C.

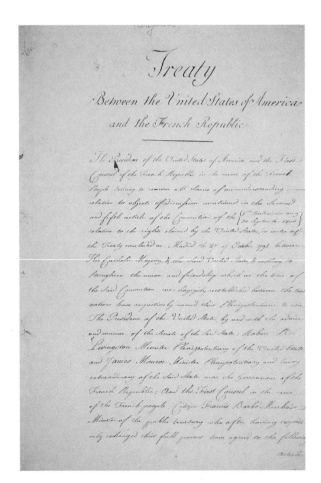

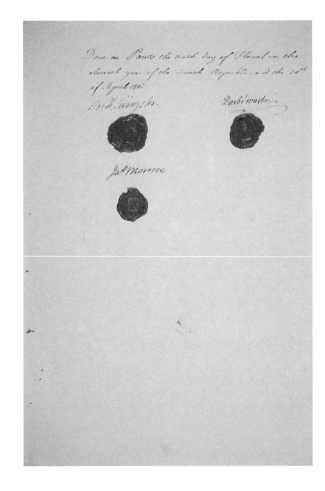

59 Louisiana Purchase

Ink on paper, wax seals
H: 36 x L: 24 cm. (14 x 9½")
Ministère des Affaires Etrangères, Paris

Original copy of the treaty in English; the French version
  has been lost

After the Treaty of Paris in 1763, France had to hand Louisiana over to Spain. In 1800, after the victory of Marengo gave Bonaparte a foothold in Italy, he negotiated with the Spanish Bourbons to have Spain return Louisiana to France. In exchange, the Kingdom of Etruria would be created and given to the brother of the Queen of Spain. This exchange was the object of a secret treaty signed at San Ildefonso on October 1, 1800. Two years later, on October 2, 1802, the treaty was ratified in the Council Chamber of Malmaison and Louisiana again became a French possession.

After much discussion and negotiation at Malmaison, Bonaparte first thought to send the French army to occupy the colony. But given the reactions of the American government and the risk that war would again break out with England, he decided to sell Louisiana for 60 million francs, plus 20 million francs in indemnities (roughly $15,000,000). The official pact was signed in Paris on April 30, 1803, by President Jefferson's two envoys, Robert Livingston and James Monroe (later the third President of the United States).

As a result of this purchase, the United States doubled in size, since the Louisiana Territory included the states of Arkansas, Colorado, Iowa, Kansas, Louisiana, Minnesota, Missouri, Montana, Nebraska, New Mexico, North Dakota, Oklahoma, South Dakota, Texas, and Wyoming. By selling Louisiana, Napoleon made the United States one of the biggest countries in the world and opened up the west.

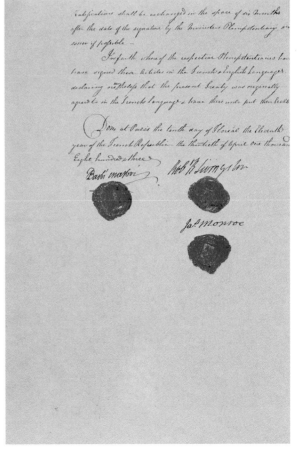

60

61

62

63

63 The Emperor's Coronation Robes

Georges Malbeste (1754-1843) and Jean-Baptiste-Michel
  Dupreel (active 1787-1828), after Charles Percier
  (1764-1838)
Copper engraving from the Coronation Book
H: 40 x L: 23.5 cm. (15¾ x 9¼")
Musée National du Château de Malmaison,
  MM 40-47-1009

Napoleon wore these official coronation robes in
commemorative portraits, notably those of Gérard.

60 The Coronation Procession on the Pont-Neuf

Jacques Bertaux
Oil on canvas
H: 94 x L: 124 cm. (37 x 48⁷/₈")
Musée Carnavalet, Paris, P 2243
Purchase, 1984

After leaving the Tuileries Palace, the coronation procession crossed the Seine River on
the Pont-Neuf and turned onto the Île de la
Cité, passing in front of the Palais de Justice
before arriving at Notre-Dame Cathedral. All
along its route, the imperial carriage, preceded
by Mamelukes and heralds, was acclaimed
by the crowds.

61 Coronation of the Emperor and the Empress

Jacques-Louis David (1748-1825)
Gouache on paper glued on canvas
H: 27.5 x L: 42.5 cm. (10⁷/₈ x 16¾")
Signed: DAVID FACIEBAT
Musée du Louvre, Paris, Département des Peintures, RF 2150
Acquired in 1925

On May 18, 1804, a decree entrusted the government of the Republic to a hereditary Emperor.
After convincing the Pope to come to Paris, the coronation ceremony took place in Notre-
Dame Cathedral on December 2, 1804. David chose to represent the moment when Napoleon,
who was already wearing the crown of laurel leaves, was about to crown Josephine. The
huge version in the Louvre (H: 629 x W: 979 cm; 20' 7½" x 32' 1½") was ordered by the
Emperor most probably in September 1804. It was completed in November 1807.

62 Napoleon in His Coronation Robes

François-Pascal, baron Gérard (1770-1837)
Oil on canvas, 1805
H: 223 x L: 143 cm. (87¾ x 56¼")
Musée National du Château de Versailles, MV 5321

Napoleon ordered the original version from the painter in 1805. The work was so successful
that Gérard made several other copies (at least ten copies are known). The Emperor
is wearing his coronation robes, of which only the tunic, the gold-fringed silk sash and
the sword have survived (Château of Fontainebleau).

64 Napoleon's Coronation Saddle

Silk velvet, red leather, silver gilt, 1804
H: 67 x L: 92 x W: 63 cm. (26 3/8 x 36 x 25")
Musée de l'Armée, Paris, Ca 21

Napoleon's horse was also in the coronation procession, with this saddle on its back. The saddle blanket, stirrups and stirrup straps have also survived. The saddle was exhibited in the Musée des Souverains, which Napoleon III created in the Louvre during the Second Empire, and was later moved to the Musée de l'Armée.

65 The Emperor Leaving the Tuileries Palace

François-Nicolas-Barthélémy Dequevauviller (1745-circa 1807),
    after Jean-Baptiste Isabey (1767-1855) and Pierre-François-
    Léonard Fontaine (1762-1853)
Copper engraving from the Coronation Book
H: 37.5 x L: 51.5 cm. (14¾ x 20¼″)
Musée National du Château de Malmaison, MM 40-47-1002

At ten o'clock, the Emperor left his apartments in
the Tuileries Palace to enter the carriage in which
the Empress and Princes Joseph and Louis were
already waiting.

66 The Emperor Arriving at Notre-Dame

Jean-Baptiste-Michel Dupreel (active 1787-1828), after
    Jean-Baptiste Isabey (1767-1855) and Pierre-François-
    Léonard Fontaine (1762-1853)
Copper engraving from the Coronation Book
H: 37.5 x L: 51.5 cm. (14¾ x 20¼″)
Musée National du Château de Malmaison, MM 40-47-1003

After crossing the Pont-Neuf, the imperial procession
arrived in front of Notre-Dame Cathedral. The architect
Fontaine built a series of Gothic-style galleries along
the facade to create a covered walkway between the
cathedral doors and the archbishop's residence.

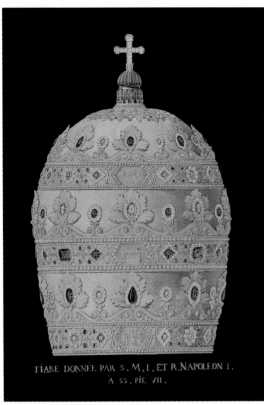

TIARE DONNÉE PAR S. M. I. ET R. NAPOLÉON I. À SS. PIE VII.

67 Sketch of Tiara of Pius VII Presented by Napoleon

Etienne Nitot (died 1809)
Gouache, circa 1804
H: 84 x L: 68 cm. (33 x 26¾″)
Musée Chaumet, Paris

This sketch provides the only opportunity we have to glimpse the tiara's original splendor; after the fall of the Empire, its precious stones and Napoleonic reliefs were removed. The jeweler Etienne Nitot worked with the goldsmith Henry August, who made the tiara. Nitot kept the sketch, which now belongs to the museum of the jewelry firm he founded, Chaumet.

68 Bust of Pope Pius VII

Antonio Canova (1757-1822)
Marble
H: 59 x W: 50 cm. (23¼ x 21³/₈″)
Vatican Museum

Barnabas Chiaramonti (1742-1823) was elected Pope under the name of Pius VII in 1800 and had the questionable privilege of ruling at the same time as Napoleon. Even though Pius VII had agreed to the Concordat, which ended the conflict with the Church of France (1802), and had later traveled to crown Napoleon in Paris (1804), he vehemently opposed the Emperor's imperialistic ambitions. The struggle led to the annexation of the Papal States by the Empire (1809) and the imprisonment of the Holy Father (1809-1814). The papacy ultimately profited from its opposition to the Empire, and the end of Pius VII's reign was more peaceful.

PIVS VII

Couronne de Charlemagne.

69 Sketch of Crown Commissioned by Napoleon to Resemble Charlemagne's

Etienne Nitot (died 1809)
Gouache, circa 1804
H: 84 x L: 67 cm. (33 x 26³⁄₈″)
Musée Chaumet, Paris

Napoleon wanted to associate his dynasty with Charlemagne, and had insignia restored or created (the originals had been destroyed during the French Revolution) which recalled the Emperor of the West, who ruled from 800 to 814. Considering himself the Great Emperor's successor, Napoleon commissioned a crown which was inspired by a medieval monument in Aachen representing Charlemagne. The crown itself was made by the goldsmith Biennais who worked with the jeweler Nitot. It is now in the Louvre.

70 Head of Napoleon

Jacques-Louis David (1748-1825)
Oil on wood
H: 43 x L: 36 cm. (17 x 14″)
Fondation Dosne-Thiers, Musée Frédéric Masson, Paris, Inv. 1346

Also shown page 45

The Emperor is wearing the gold laurel wreath by Biennais he crowned himself with in Notre-Dame Cathedral. The crown was made of 44 large gold laurel leaves and 12 smaller ones. It was melted down during the Restoration, except for one leaf which is in the collection of the Château of Fontainebleau. The head is similar to the one in the large standing portrait the City of Genoa ordered from David, and which the Emperor refused.

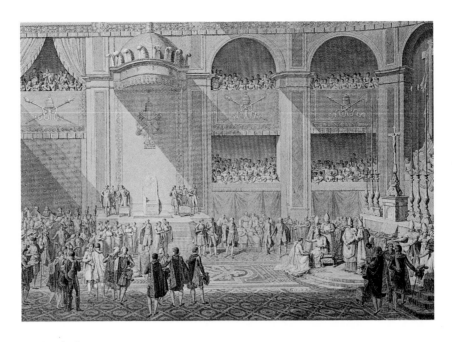

71 Anointing

Rémi-Henri-Joseph Delvaux (1748-1823), after Jean-Baptiste Isabey (1767-1855) and
  Pierre-François-Léonard Fontaine (1762-1853)
Copper engraving from the Coronation Book
H: 36.5 x L: 53 cm. (14 3/8 x 20 7/8″)
Musée National du Château de Malmaison, MM 40-47-1004

This was the moment when the Sovereign Pontiff rose from his throne and
from his footstool anointed the Emperor and the Empress who were kneeling
in front of him.

72 Coronation of the Emperor

Jacques Lavallée (1745-circa 1807), after Jean-Baptiste Isabey (1767-1855) and
  Pierre-François-Léonard Fontaine (1762-1853)
Copper engraving from the Coronation Book
H: 87.5 x L: 106.5 cm. (34½ x 42″)
Musée National du Château de Malmaison, MM 40-47-1005

After anointing the Emperor and blessing the imperial symbols of power, the
Pope gave them to the Emperor, who put them on and crowned himself. Napoleon
then crowned Josephine who knelt before him (this is the moment the painter
David chose to represent).

73 Offertory

Jean-Jacques-Franǫis Simonet, after Jean-Baptiste Isabey (1767-1855) and
  Pierre-François-Léonard Fontaine (1762-1853)
Copper engraving from the Coronation Book
H: 37 x L: 53 cm. (14½ x 20⅞″)
Musée National du Château de Malmaison, MM 40-47-1006

During the offertory, the Emperor and the Empress rose from their thrones
to participate.

74 The Emperor's Oath

Jean-Louis-Charles Pauquet (1759-circa 1824) and Jean-Louis Delignon (1755-circa 1830),
  after Jean-Baptiste Isabey (1767-1855) and Pierre-François-Léonard Fontaine
  (1762-1853)
Copper engraving from the Coronation Book
H: 37 x L: 52 cm. (14½ x 20½″)
Musée National du Château de Malmaison, MM 40-47-1007

Seated on his throne, the Emperor took the constitutional oath and placed his
hand on the Gospels which were presented by the Court Chaplain.

75 The Empress' Coronation Robes
Pierre Audouin (1768-1822), after Jean-Baptiste Isabey
(1767-1855) and Charles Percier (1764-1838)
Copper engraving from the Coronation Book
H: 40 x L: 23 cm. (15¾ x 9")
Musée National du Château de Malmaison, MM 40-47-1011

76 The Empress' Coronation Day Dress
Jean-François Ribault (1767-1820), after Jean-Baptiste Isabey
(1767-1855) and Charles Percier (1764-1838)
Copper engraving from the Coronation Book
H: 40 x L: 23.5 cm. (15¾ x 9¼")
Musée National du Château de Malmaison, MM 40-47-1012

**77 Slippers worn by Josephine
at the Coronation**
Satin with gold embroidery, leather
H: 70 x L: 23 x W: 5 cm. (27½ x 9 x 2" or U.S. ladies size 5)
Musée des Arts de la Mode et de Textile, Paris, 15.110 A B
Gift of Madame Amédée Loiseau, 1908

78 The Emperor's Coronation Day Costume

Jean-François Ribault (1767-1820), after Jean-Baptiste Isabey
  (1767-1855) and Charles Percier (1764-1838)
Copper engraving from the Coronation Book
H: 30 x L: 22 cm. (11¾ x 8⅝″)
Musée National du Château de Malmaison, MM 40-47-1010

Napoleon wore this costume on the day of the Coronation
before and after the ceremony in Notre-Dame Cathedral.

80 Silk Stockings worn by Napoleon at the Coronation

Silk with gold embroidery
H: 82 x L: 15 cm. (32¼ x 5⅞″)
Musée des Arts de la Mode et du Textile, Paris, 32 179 A B
Gift of Madame G. Jacques, *née* Le Maréchal, 1934

Napoleon wore this pair of silk stockings at the Coronation.
Josephine later gave them to her friend Fortunée Hamelin,
who was as famous for her beauty as
for the number of her
conquests.

79 Coronation Portrait of Napoleon as King of Italy

Andrea Appiani (1754-1817)
Oil on canvas, 1805
H: 98.5 x L: 74.5 cm. (38¾ x 29¼″)
Signed: A. APPIA...
Musée National de î'lle d'Aix, Fondation Gourgaud, MG A 881

Also shown page 21

Already President of the Italian Republic, Napoleon decided a month
after his Coronation to accept the crown of Italy as well. The Coronation
took place in the Milan Cathedral on May 26, 1805, in the presence
of the Empress who only attended the ceremony. On June 7, 1805,
the Emperor named Prince Eugène, the son of the Empress
Josephine, Viceroy of Italy.

THRONE ROOM

When he became Emperor, Napoleon asked his architects to build a throne room for the official audiences he would have to give. Four of Napoleon's thrones have survived the ravages of time--those from the Tuileries Palace and from Fontainebleau are kept at Fontainebleau. The throne from the Senate is still there, and the one he used in the Legislative Assembly now belongs to the Musée des Arts Décoratifs.

81 Throne Room at the Tuileries

Charles Percier (1764-1838) and Pierre-François-Léonard Fontaine (1762-1853)
Ink and watercolor sketch
H: 57.5 x L: 53 cm. (22 5/8 x 20 7/8")
Private collection, Paris

This is a sketch of the Emperor's throne for the Tuileries Palace. Napoleonic motifs such as the eagle, the Legion of Honor and the bees are readily apparent.

82 Throne from the Legislative Assembly

François-Honoré-George Jacob-Desmalter (1770-1841), after a drawing by Bernard Poyet (1742-1824)
Gilt wood, velvet, gold embroidery, 1804
H: 160 x L: 110 x W: 82 cm. (63 x 43¼ x 32¼")
Musée des Arts Décoratifs, Paris, Inv. 14421

The Legislative Assembly, one of the two legislative bodies with the Senate, was to meet in the Emperor's presence. It was therefore necessary to make a throne for the sovereign and a ceremonial armchair for the Empress as rapidly as possible. Jacob-Desmalter delivered this throne in the fall of 1804. Only the front part was modified for King Louis XVIII. The embroidery was created by Picot, the Emperor's official embroiderer.

83 Throne Room Carpet

Period replica of the carpet in the Throne Room in the Tuileries
   Palace given by Napoleon to the King of Saxony in 1809
Manufacture de la Savonnerie
Wool, 1807-1809
L: 780 x W: 640 cm. (25′ 4 7/8″ x 21′)
Musée National du Château de Malmaison, MM 40-47-8112
Gift of Mrs. Helen Fahnestock-Hubbard, 1926

When Napoleon married Marie-Louise, the original carpet in the Throne
Room in the Tuileries Palace was replaced by a huge three-piece carpet from the
Manufacture de la Savonnerie. It had originally been ordered in 1806 for the
State Council Chamber in the Tuileries. It was designed by the architect François
Debret (1783-1850), a student of Percier's. A replica of one of the side panels
was woven between 1807 and 1809, and then presented to the King of Saxony
when he visited Paris on December 5, 1809. Put up for sale after the fall of the
Saxon monarchy in 1918, it was bought for the Château of Malmaison by a
wealthy American, Mrs. Fahnestock-Hubbard. It is the only carpet known to
historians which still has all the emblems of the Empire and the letter N (the
other throne room carpets were altered during the Restoration).

84 Tapestry with the Arms of the French Empire

Manufacture des Gobelins
Wool and silk, 1809
H: 325 x L: 235 cm. (128 x 92½")
Mobilier National, Paris, GOB 23

Ordered for the Emperor's official study in the Tuileries Palace, this panel is the only one of the six Gobelins tapestries made for the room which has survived. Designed by Jacques-Louis de La Hamayde de Saint-Ange (1780-1860), it represents the emblems of the Empire—the eagle, the Legion of Honor and the bees. It was woven over a period of two years, between January 26, 1809, and January 12, 1811.

85 Josephine's Armchair from the Tribune of the Legislative Assembly

François-Honoré-George Jacob-Desmalter (1770-1841)
Gilt wood, velvet, 1804
H: 105 x L: 68 x W: 48 cm. (41¼ x 26¾ x 18⅞")
Musée des Arts Décoratifs, Paris, Inv. 14422

The Empress watched the sessions of the Legislative Assembly from the official tribune. In 1804, Jacob-Desmalter delivered this ceremonial armchair, similar to those he had made for the throne rooms of the Tuileries and Saint Cloud Palaces.

86 Standing Candelabra

François-Honoré-George Jacob-Desmalter (1770-1841), after a drawing by
  Alexandre-Théodore Brongniart (1739-1813)
Gilt wood
H: 210 x L: 65 cm. (82 ⁵⁄₈ x 25 ⁵⁄₈")
Mobilier National, Paris, GML 3698

In 1809, Jacob-Desmalter delivered six twelve-branch candelabra for the
Throne Room in the Tuileries Palace to replace the two made in 1806. These
candelabra were thought to have been lost and were only recently discovered
by Madame Chantal Coural, Conseiller technique at the Mobilier National in
Paris. This is the first time they have been on public display since the fall of
the Second Empire in 1870.

87 Josephine's Swan Armchairs

François-Honoré-Georges Jacob-Desmalter
Wood, gold, red silk velvet, gold thread, circa 1804
H: 77 x L: 66 x W: 51 cm. (30¼ x 26 x 20")
Musée National du Château de Malmaison, MM 40-47-942/943

These armchairs were part of an ensemble from Saint Cloud which included
a sofa, four armchairs and four chairs. Only the four armchairs, now in the
collection of the Château of Malmaison, have survived. Delivered for the
boudoir of the Empress Josephine in the Palace of Saint Cloud, these chairs
were some of the most extraordinary pieces of furniture made by Jacob-
Desmalter. They were designed by the architect Percier, who gave them
such a graceful shape that they have always been associated with
Josephine. This is the first time they have been exhibited re-upholstered
as they were originally.

88 Blue Damask Decorated with ''N'' and Shields

Grand Frères, after a drawing by Alexandre-Théodore
Brongniart (1739-1813)
Silk, 1808-1809
H: 140 x L: 54 cm. (55 1/8 x 21¼")
Mobilier National, Paris, Inv. 62 - GMTC 99/1

Grand Frères, which took over the Pernon workshop,
delivered this hanging for the Salon of the Meudon
Palace, the summer residence of Napoleon's son, the
King of Rome. The house was unfortunately burned
down in 1871 during the Franco-Prussian War. This is
the only hanging which still has the Emperor's initial—
the others were altered during the Restoration. It was
designed by the architect Alexandre-Théodore Brongniart,
who was Inspector of the Imperial Furniture Storehouse
from 1806 until his death and who initiated several
important imperial projects.

89 Blue and Silver Brocade with Myrtle and Ivy Leaves

Camille Pernon (1753-1808)
Silk, silver thread, 1802-1803
H: 265 x L: 162 cm. (104¼ x 63¾")
Mobilier National, Paris, Inv. 1 - GMMP 139

In 1802, in an effort to stimulate industry in Lyon, the First Consul ordered several silk wall hangings from Camille Pernon for the Palace of Saint Cloud. This magnificent brocade was to be hung in the Salon of Josephine, but was not put up until 1808, when it was used to decorate the Empress' Salon in the Tuileries Palace. The pattern was suggested by the famous designer Jean-Démosthène Dugourc (1749-1825).

90 Flower and Bird Embroidered White Satin

Bissardon, Cousin and Bony
Silk, 1811-1812
H: 330 x L: 520 cm. (10' 6⅞" x 17')
Mobilier National, Paris, Inv. 53 - GMMP 28 and 29

In 1810, Napoleon was planning to make Versailles his principal residence. Since the Lyon silk industry was in the midst of a major crisis, the Emperor decided to place a large order for silk hangings. The total order was for almost 50 miles of silk! Delivered between 1811 and 1813, much of the silk was never used during the Empire, and some of it is almost like new even today. This richly embroidered satin, designed by Jean-François Bony, was made for the private salon of the Empress Marie-Louise in the Versailles Palace. Never used, it is still in pristine condition.

92

93

91 Napoleon Receiving Representatives of the Army after his Coronation

Manufacture des Gobelins, after Gioachino Serangeli
(1768-1852)
Wool and silk, 1809-1815
H: 330 x L: 195 cm. (10′ 6⅞″ x 6′ 3¼″)
Mobilier National, Paris, GMTT 250

Knowing that Louis XIV had ordered tapestries representing highlights of his reign from the Manufacture des Gobelins, Napoleon decided to do the same and ordered sixteen tapestries in 1806. The fall of the Empire ended the project, but several panels had already been woven. This tapestry was ordered in 1806, after a painting by Gioachino Serangeli. Initially, it was to decorate the Salon of Mars in the Palace of Versailles, and later the official study of the Emperor in the Tuileries Palace. Weaving began on November 20, 1809 and stopped on June 30, 1815–15 days after Napoleon's defeat at Waterloo.

92 Meeting of the Emperors Napoleon and Alexander at Tilsit

Manufacture des Gobelins, after René Berthon (1778-1859)
Wool and silk, 1811-1815
H: 328 x L: 128 cm. (10′ 6¼″ x 4′ 1½″)
Musée National du Château de Malmaison, MM 40-47-8117

This panel represents part of a painting by René Berthon.

93 Napoleon Gives a Saber to the Military Chief of Alexandria, July 1798

Manufacture des Gobelins, after François-Henri Mulard
(1769-1850)
Wool and silk, 1812-1815
H: 230 x L: 113 cm. (90½ x 44½″)
Musée National du Château de Malmaison, MM 40-47-8405

This panel represents the left side of a painting by François-Henri Mulard. The Emperor ordered it for the Throne Room in the Tuileries Palace. It was exhibited in the Salon of 1808 and today is in the collection of the Château of Versailles.

94 Napoleon Receives the Keys to Vienna, November 13, 1805

Manufacture des Gobelins, after Anne-Louis Girodet
(1778-1824)
Wool and silk, 1810-1815
H: 335 x L: 172 cm. (10' 8¼" x 5' 5 ⅜")
Musée National du Château de Malmaison, MM 40-47-8118

This panel represents the left side of the painting by Anne-Louis Girodet. It was ordered for the Tuileries Palace and subsequently exhibited in the Salon of 1808. Today, it is in the collection of the Château of Versailles.

95 Napoleon Receives Finkenstein, the Persian Ambassador, April 27, 1807

Manufacture des Gobelins, after François-Henri Mulard
(1769-1850)
Wool and silk, 1812-1815
H: 310 x L: 110 cm. (10' 1⅜" x 3' 5")
Musée National du Château de Malmaison, MM 40-47-8407

A painting by François-Henri Mulard inspired this panel, which was ordered for the Throne Room in the Tuileries Palace. Today, the canvas is in the collection of the Château of Versailles.

96 Gros de Tours White Silk Decorated with the Attributes of the Arts and the Sciences

Lacostat and Trollier
Silk, 1810-1812
H: 455 x L: 430 cm. (14′ 7⅝″ x 14′)
Mobilier National, Paris, Inv. 37 - GMMP 1058 and 884/1

Made for the second Salon in the great apartments of
the Palace of Meudon, this hanging was also designed
by the architect Alexandre-Théodore Brongniart (1739-
1813), who added the attributes of war, trade, the arts
and the sciences.

97 Pair of Medici Vases
98 Manufacture de Sèvres, panels painted by
   Jacques-François-Joseph Swebach (1769-1823)
   Sèvres porcelain, 1812
   H: 68 x D: 48 cm. (26¾ x 18⅞")
   Musée National du Château de Malmaison,
      MMD 115 and 116
   Loan of the Musée National du Château de
      Compiègne, 1969

During the Empire, the Sèvres porcelain factory continued
to produce vases, dishes and toilet articles almost
exclusively for the Emperor's residences. The Egyptian
decoration of these Medici vases was the work
of the architect Alexandre-Théodore
Brongniart (1739-1813), who designed
many objects for the Sèvres porcelain
factory. The two panels, painted in 1812
by Jacques-François-Joseph Swebach,
represent a ''View of Egypt and an
Arab Camp'' and a ''View of Poland
and a Cossack Bivouac.'' Originally in
the Tuileries Palace, these vases were
moved to the Salon of Malmaison
during the Second Empire.

99 Josephine's Secretary and Letter File

Martin-Guillaume Biennais (1764-1843)
Wood and gilt bronze, circa 1805-1810
H: 58 x L: 52.5 x W: 45.5 cm. (22 ⁷/₈ x 20 ⁵/₈ x 18″)
Fondation Napoléon, Paris
Acquisition, 1991

In all her palaces, the Empress liked to keep her mail
and personal papers rolled up in scrolls in letter files
such as this. Inside the file, there is a secret drawer, and
the keyhole is hidden by a medallion with the Empress'
coat of arms. In 1814, this file was in the boudoir of the
Empress in the Château of Malmaison, together with a
second copy in mahogany, which has fortunately been
returned to its original location in Malmaison.

100 Bust of Napoleon

Manufacture de Sèvres, after Antoine-Denis Chaudet
  (1763-1810)
Biscuit, 1807
H: 47 x L: 27 cm. (18½ x 10⅝″)
Musée National du Château de Malmaison, MMDO 223
Osiris donation, 1912

One of the functions of the Sèvres porcelain
factory was to make effigies of the sovereign,
most of which were created for official gifts.
In 1805, Antoine-Denis Chaudet provided the
factory with the model of the bust of Napoleon
he had sculpted during the Consulate. It was
used as the official portrait of the Emperor until
at least 1810. This copy is signed: A.B.7.A.7—
the initials of the sculptor/repairer Alexandre
Brachard (1775-1843)—and dated: April 7, 1807.

101 Sèvres Plate from the Olympic Service, Apollo and Daphne

Manufacture de Sèvres
Porcelain, 1805
D: 24 cm. (9½")
Musée National de Céramique, Sèvres, Inv. 1790

Made in 1805-1806, this 140-piece service was given by Napoleon to Czar Alexander of Russia in 1807. The subject is the metamorphosis of Daphne into a laurel tree. The scene was painted by Madame Jacquotot, the most famous female porcelain painter at the beginning of the nineteenth century.

102 Sèvres Plate from Napoleon's Personal Service with a View of Mainz

Manufacture de Sèvres
Porcelain, 1805
D: 24 cm. (9½")
Fondation Napoléon, Paris
Purchase, 1991

The Emperor's personal service, also called the Headquarters Service, is the most famous set of dishes manufactured by the Sèvres factory during the Empire. Each of the 72 dessert plates presents a different subject. Napoleon took 60 of these plates to Saint Helena with him, but the set was broken up after his death. The view of Mainz on this plate was painted by the landscape artist Nicolas-Antoine Lebel (1780-1849).

103 Sèvres Plate from the Various Scenes Service, View of the Palace of Saint Cloud

Manufacture de Sèvres
Porcelain, 1815
D: 24 cm. (9½″)
Musée National de Céramique, Sèvres, Inv. 1815

In addition to the Emperor's personal service, the Sèvres factory made a second dessert service, beginning in 1812 and continuing during the Restoration. The number of plates was to be unlimited, and most of them are today in the collection of the Château of Fontainebleau. This view of Saint Cloud was painted by Jean-Baptiste-Langlacé.

104 Sèvres Plate from the Egyptian Service

Manufacture de Sèvres
Porcelain, 1811
D: 23.7 cm. (9⅜″)
Musée National de Céramique, Sèvres, Inv. 26308
Purchased with the help of the Fondation Napoléon, 1989

The Egyptian service, made in 1811-1812, was delivered to the Empress Josephine who did not like it and therefore refused it. In 1818, it was finally given by Louis XVIII to the Duke of Wellington with a note that said: ''Do little gifts keep friendship alive.'' Most of the scenes were painted by Jacques-François-Joseph Swebach (1769-1823).

105 Sèvres Plate from the Gold Trim Service

Manufacture de Sèvres
Porcelain, 1810
D: 23.7 cm. (9⅜")
Musée National de Céramique, Sèvres, Inv. 7920/4
Saint-Aubin bequest

Each of the plates in this service has a gold border, and
the center is decorated with mythological scenes, landscapes or flowers. Begun in 1805, the Sèvres factory
continued to make this service during the Restoration,
thus providing work for the factory's artists between
larger orders. On this plate, the painter Drouet
reproduced a work by Van Spaendonck.

106 Sèvres Plate from the Greek Service, the Medici Venus

Manufacture de Sèvres
Porcelain, 1810
D: 23.8 cm. (9 3/8″)
Musée National de Céramique, Sèvres, Inv. 1809
Saint-Aubin bequest

Napoleon gave this service, sometimes called the Cameo Service, to his uncle, Cardinal Fesch, in 1811 to commemorate the baptism of the King of Rome. This replacement plate, which has never previously left the factory, was painted by Jean-Marie Degault.

107 **Champagne Glass Engraved with the Initial of the Emperor Napoleon**

Crystal
H: 20 x D: 7 cm. (7⁷/₈ x 2¾")
Musée National du Château de Malmaison, MM 40-47-2916
Gift of Colonel Jourdan, 1938

108 **Champagne Glass Engraved with the Initial of the Empress Josephine**

Crystal
H: 20 x D: 7 cm. (7⁷/₈ x 2¾")
Musée National du Château de Malmaison, MM 40-47-196
Gift of the Empress Eugénie, 1906

All the crystal for the imperial palaces was made by the Montcenis factory which, after 1806, was called the *Manufacture des cristaux de S. M. l'Impératrice.*

109 **Bronze Clock Representing Diogenes and Napoleon**

Claude Galle (1759-1815)
Gilt bronze and sea-green marble, 1806
H: 87 x L: 67 x W: 35 cm. (34¼ x 26³/₈ x 13 3/4")
Musée National du Château de Malmaison, MM 40-47-8389
Purchase, 1938

This monumental clock was presented by Galle at the industrial exhibition of 1806. It was a tremendous success, basically because of the allegory it represents—by the light of his lantern, Diogenes, who spent his life looking for an honest man, finally finds Napoleon, crowned by victory. On the base, on each side of the Empire coat of arms, the figures of Fame and History record Napoleon's heroic deeds, while the Seine and the Tiber Rivers symbolize the union of the French Empire and the Kingdom of Italy.

Monuments of Paris

Victoire-Jean Nicolle (1754-1826)
Watercolor on paper, circa 1810
H: 6.7 x L: 11.7 cm. (2 ⁵/₈ x 4 ⁵/₈")
Signed: V.J. NICOLLE PINXIT
Musée National du Château de Malmaison, MM 40-47-9043-6/21/38/42/45/46/47/50
Gift of Mr. and Mrs. John Jaffé, 1933

Among the most valuable works of art in the collection of the Château of Malmaison is this series of watercolors kept in a red leather case with the coat of arms of the Empress Marie-Louise. The album was created to show the new Empress, who came from Austria, the principal monuments of the capital where she was going to reside and to show her the projects undertaken by Napoleon. It remained in the Hapsburg family after the death of Marie-Louise, until it was acquired by Mr. and Mrs. John Jaffé, who gave it to the museum with more than 700 books from imperial collections.

110 View of the Facade of the Legislative Assembly
MM 40-47-9043-50

The former residence of the Bourbon-Condé at the end of the Concorde Bridge had been the seat of the Council of the Five Hundred during the Revolution. It became the seat of the Legislative Assembly, one of the four assemblies of the new government. The architect Bernard Poyet (1742-1824) put a monumental Greek portico on the former facade. The cornerstone was laid in 1806.

111 View of the Invalides, from the North Side
MM 40-47-9043-46

The Invalides was built by Louis XIV to serve as a hospital for wounded soldiers. Napoleon I was buried under the dome of the church in 1840. In front of the structure, the Emperor had a fountain built in 1804 on top of which was the lion of Saint Mark, brought from Venice in 1797. The lion was returned to the Venetians in 1815.

112 View of the Bellique Column, Place Vendôme

MM 40-47-9043-47

The Bellique Column was the name sometimes given to the Column of the Great Army or the Austerlitz Column.

113 Views of the Place de la Concorde, Formerly Louis XV, and of the Crown's Furniture Storehouse and of the Ministry of the Navy

MM 40-47-9043-45

The Place de la Concorde, designed by the architect Jacques-Ange Gabriel (1698-1772), was built between 1757 and 1772. During the Revolution, the equestrian statue of Louis XV was taken down. The Luxor obelisk was not erected until 1836 under the reign of Louis-Philippe.

114 View of the Paris Town Hall and Its Square

MM 40-47-9043-42

The Paris Town Hall was built in two stages, first under the reigns of Francis I and Henry II (middle of the sixteenth century), then under those of Henry IV and Louis XIII (beginning of the seventeenth century). It was burned down during the Commune in 1871. An almost identical copy was rebuilt between 1873 and 1883.

115 View of the Gallery of the Louvre
MM 40-47-9043-21

The *Grande Galerie* was built by Henry IV at the beginning of the seventeenth century between the Louvre and the Tuileries Palace. The Gallery then housed the Napoleon Museum, now the Louvre Museum.

116 View of the Monument to the Memory of General Desaix
MM 40-47-9043-6

In 1803, on the site of the Place Dauphine, near the Palace of Justice, the First Consul inaugurated a fountain built to commemorate General Desaix who had been killed in the Battle of Marengo. In 1904, the fountain was moved to Riom in Auvergne, the city in central France where Desaix was from.

117 View of the Square and the Portal of the Basilica of Notre-Dame
MM 40-47-9043-38

Notre-Dame Cathedral was begun in 1163 and completed in 1330. It had been the site of some of the main events in the history of France before the Coronation of Napoleon by Pius VII on December 2, 1804.

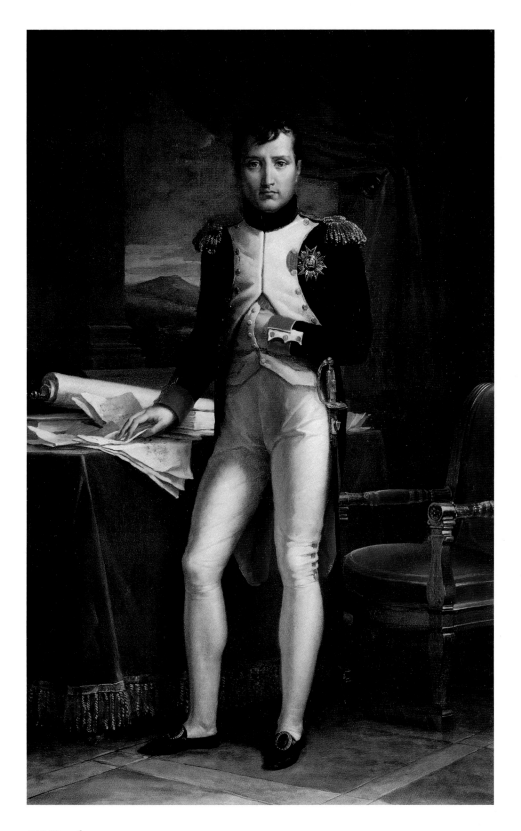

118 **Napoleon**

Attributed to François, baron Gérard (1770-1837)
Oil on canvas, circa 1812
H: 107 x L: 70.5 cm. (42 1/8 x 27¾")
Musée Napoléon, Île d'Aix, MG A 207
Gift of Baron Gourgaud

The Emperor is represented in the uniform of a colonel
of the *grenadiers à pied* of the Imperial Guard.

119

120

119 Panoramic View of the Palace of Saint Cloud

French school, nineteenth century
Watercolor and gouache on paper
H: 61 x L: 96 cm. (24 x 37¾")
Musée de L'Île de France, Château de Sceaux
Purchase, Musée Carnavalet, 1890; loan from the Musée
 Carnavalet, 1937

Bought by Queen Marie-Antoinette in 1785, the Palace
of Saint Cloud was the former residence of *Monsieur,*
the brother of Louis XIV. In 1802, it was attributed to
Bonaparte, who made it his principal residence after
the Tuileries Palace. It remained the main palace of the
rulers of France until it was burned down in 1871, and
its ruins destroyed twenty years later. Although the
painting depicts the visit of the King and Queen of
Naples in May 1830, the palace had not changed
since Napoleon lived there.

120 Palace and Gardens of the Tuileries

Etienne Bouhot (1780-1862)
Oil on canvas, 1813
H: 54 x L: 92 cm. (21¼ x 36¼")
Signed: BOUHOT 1813
Musée Carnavalet, Paris, P 1513

Three months after the coup of 18 *Brumaire,*
Bonaparte went to live in the Tuileries Palace (February
1800). He made the palace his principal residence, as
did all of France's rulers until 1870. He immediately
occupied the royal apartments on the second floor,
while Josephine took over the apartment of Marie-
Antoinette on the ground floor. The Tuileries proved to
be uncomfortable, and life there was unpleasant because
of the strict protocol. For these reasons, towards the
end of his reign, the Emperor was planning to restore
Versailles and move there.

121 Napoleon's Personal Washstand

Martin-Guillaume Biennais (1764-1843) and
 Joseph-Marie-Gabriel Genu, after Charles Percier (1764-1838)
Yew, gilt bronze, silver, 1800-1804
H: 90 x D: 47 cm. (35³/₈ x 18½")
Musée du Louvre, Paris, Département des Objets d'Art, OA 10424
Given to the government in payment of inheritance taxes, 1973

Directly inspired by antiquity, this washstand was
designed by Percier and made by Biennais, Napoleon's
official goldsmith, with the assistance of Genu. Bonaparte
used it in his bedroom in the Tuileries Palace from the
time he was First Consul to the end of the Empire. As
a personal possession, it followed Napoleon to the
Elysée Palace, where he lived after the Battle of
Waterloo, then to Saint Helena. After his death,
when his estate was divided, it was inherited
by his sister Caroline Murat. It remained in the
Murat family until it entered the Louvre.

122 View of the Château from the Park

Views of Malmaison

Ambroise-Louis Garnerey (1783-1857), after Auguste Garnerey
   (1785-1824)
Aquatint on paper, circa 1815-1820
H: 31.5 x L: 39.5 cm. (12 3/8 x 15½")
Musée National du Château de Malmaison,
   MM 40-47-4222/4223/4224/4236/4237/4254/4255/4256
Gift of Bernard Franck

In 1820, Auguste Garnerey gave Prince Eugène, the son
of the Empress Josephine, a series of twelve watercolors
representing different views of the Malmaison estate.
Eight of these scenes were engraved by his brother
Louis Garnerey and published under the reign of
Louis XVIII.

123 The Wooden Bridge Seen from the River,
near the Statue of Diana

124 **The Park Seen from the Château**

125 **The Bergerie**

126 **View of the Château
from the Stone Bridge**

127 **The Stucco Salon in the Greenhouse**

128 **The Milk Farm of Saint Cucufa**

129 **The Neptune Fountain by Puget**

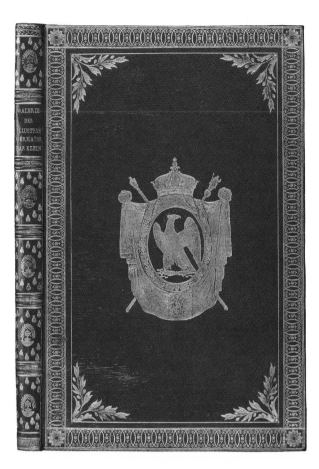

130 *Galerie historique des illustres Germains*

Binding attributed to René Simier (died 1826)
Paper, red leather binding, 1806; folio volume
H: 46 x L: 31 cm. (18 ⅛ x 12¼″)
Musée National du Château de Malmaison, MM 40-47-6473
Gift of Mr. and Mrs. John Jaffé, 1933

This work by the German poet Anton von Klein
includes a biography and a portrait of illustrious
Germans. The Emperor's coat of arms decorates the
binding, and the spine is covered with imperial bees.

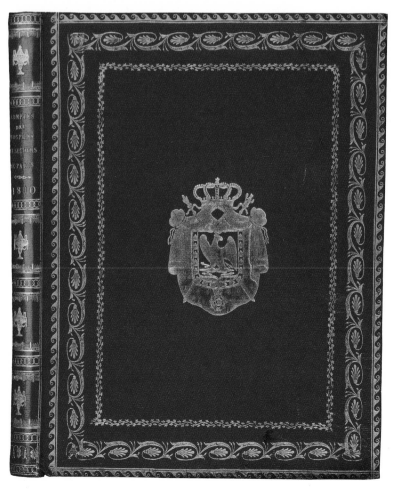

131 *Comptes des Hospices et Secours de Paris*

Binding anonymous
Paper, red leather binding, 1810; 4° volume
H: 36 x L: 23.5 cm. (14⅛ x 9¼″)
Musée National du Château de Malmaison,
  MM 40-47-6475
Gift of Mr. and Mrs. John Jaffé, 1933

This book, which lists the accounts of the
hospitals, homes and orphanages in the
department of the Seine, is magnificently
bound with the Emperor's coat of arms.

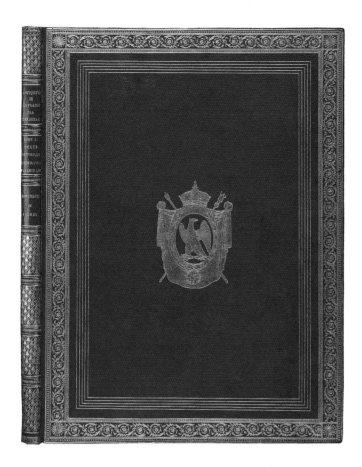

132 Antiquités de France

Binding anonymous
Paper, red leather binding, 1804; grand folio volume
H: 46 x L: 31 cm. (18 ⅛ x 12¼")
Musée National du Château de Malmaison, MM 40-47-6758
Gift of Mr. and Mrs. John Jaffé, 1933

This work by the architect Charles-Louis Clérisseau (1722-1820) was first published in 1778; it was so successful that the famous printer Pierre Didot published a second edition in 1804. An important book, the author's designs inspired many of the period's architects.

133 Voyage dans l'Hindoustan

Binding by René Simier (died 1826)
Paper, red leather binding, 1813; 4° volume
H: 21 x L: 28 cm. (8¼ x 11")
Musée National du Château de Malmaison, MM 40-47-6711
Gift of Mr. and Mrs. John Jaffé, 1933

Viscount George Valentia wrote about his trips to India, Abyssinia and Egypt between 1802 and 1806. The book was first published in English. This French translation was bound with Empress Marie-Louise's coat of arms.

Le Promerops, à bec rouge. Pl. 6.

134 *Oiseaux dorés ou à reflets métalliques*

Binding by Jean-Claude Bozerian
Paper, red leather binding, 1802, folio volume
H: 51.5 X L: 34 cm. (20¼ x 13⅜″)
Musée National du Château de Malmaison, MM 40-47-6744
Gift of Mr. and Mrs. John Jaffé, 1933

In order to have the book itself reflect the subject matter, the
text, which was written by the naturalist Louis-Pierre Vieillot
(1748-1831), was printed in gold. The color engravings of the
birds were made from drawings by Jean-Baptiste Audebert
(1759-1800). Only twenty copies were printed of this two-
volume folio edition, and only twelve were printed in gold.

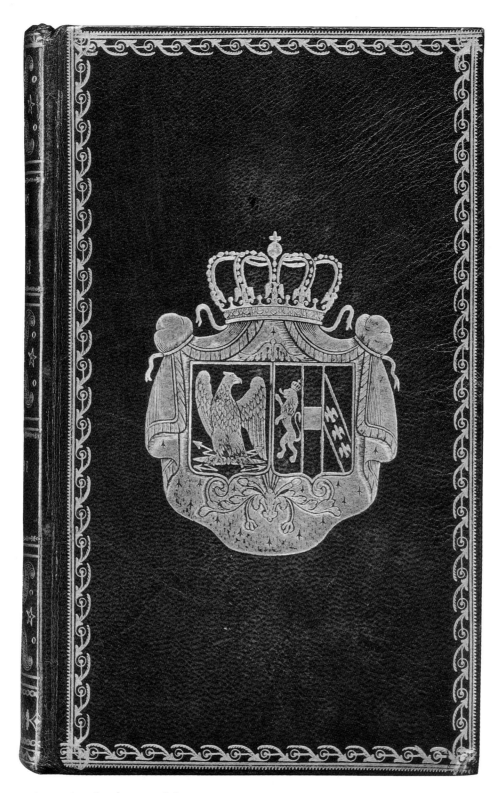

135 *Sermons du Père Bourdaloue*
de la Compagnie de Jésus

Binding attributed to René Simier (died 1826)
Paper, green leather binding, 1707-1721; 8° volume
H: 20 x L: 13 cm. (7⅞ x 5⅛")
Musée National du Château de Malmaison, MM 40-47-6759
Gift of Mr. and Mrs. John Jaffé, 1933

Sixteen volumes of sermons by Father Bourdaloue, S.J. were
published in the eighteenth century and were bound for the
Empress Marie-Louise with her coat of arms in green leather.
This was an exception, as most of the other volumes in the
collection were bound in red leather.

136 *Habit à la française* Worn by Napoleon

Chevallier (tailor) and Augustin-François-André Picot
 (embroiderer)
Red velvet, satin, gold and silver thread, 1806
H: 108 x L: 30 cm. (42½ x 11¾″)
Musée National du Château de Fontainebleau, MS 182-2

Napoleon had three red dress coats, all of which were
embroidered by Picot, after sketches by Isabey. The first
was part of his Coronation Day costume. The second,
presented here and identical to the first, was delivered
in 1806. The third was made in 1810 for his wedding
with Marie-Louise. Today, all three are in the collections
of the Château of Fontainebleau.

137 Sketch of Napoleon's Court Sword

François-Regnault Nitot
Gouache on paper, 1811
H: 113 x L: 81 cm. (44½ x 31⅞″)
Musée Chaumet, Paris

The imperial sword and its belt were delivered by the
younger Nitot in 1812 and embellished with several
jewels, such as the famous 136-carat Regent diamond,
which is today in the Louvre.

138 Court Sword of Napoleon

Martin-Guillaume Biennais (1764-1843)
Vermeil, steel, leather, circa 1810
H: 92.5 x L: 10.5 cm. (36⅜ x 4⅛″)
Musée National du Château de Fontainebleau, N 208
Acquired from Prince Napoleon, 1979

This type of sword, designed by Biennais, was for the
Emperor's personal use. Four others have survived,
with slight variations.

139 Uniform of a Colonel of the *Chasseurs à cheval* of the Imperial Guard
Worn by Napoleon

Lejeune
Fabric, circa 1813-1815
H: 100 x L: 66 cm. (39 3/8 x 26″)
Musée de Sens

Accustomed to wearing a simple colonel's uniform, Napoleon often wore either that of the *grendaiers à pied* of the Guard or that of the *chasseurs à cheval* of the Guard. Although many uniforms were made for Napoleon during the Empire, very few of them have survived. In fact, only four *chasseur* and two *grenadier* uniforms remain. This one was taken to Saint Helena and given by the Emperor to the Mameluke Ali who served him faithfully during his exile. When he died, Ali bequeathed the uniform to the City of Sens, together with other memorabilia of the Emperor.

140 Empress Josephine

Jean-Baptiste, baron Regnault (1754-1829)
Oil on canvas
H: 84 x L: 72 cm. (33 x 28 ³/₈")
Fondation Dosne-Thiers, Musée Frédéric Masson, Paris,
 Inv. 48

This portrait was only recently identified as being of the
Empress Josephine. Changing the jewels and the dress,
Regnault copied a portion of his large painting representing
the marriage of Jerome and Catherine de Württemberg
(Château of Versailles).

141 Court Dress and Train of Josephine

Attributed to the dressmaker Louis-Hippolyte Leroy
Silk, silver, crystal
H of dress: 135 cm. (53 ¹/₈"); L of train: 300 cm. (118 ¹/₈")
Musée National du Château de Malmaison, N 328
Acquired from Prince Napoleon, 1979

Josephine invested a great deal of time and money
in her wardrobe, but she did not just buy what was
fashionable—she helped launch *la mode.* Her official
dressmaker, Leroy, knew how to flatter her and
encouraged her to spend an enormous amount of
money. In 1809, the inventory of her wardrobe listed
49 official court ensembles and 676 dresses. In just
one year, Josephine ordered 136 outfits, 87 hats, 985
pairs of gloves, and 520 pairs of shoes!

142 Diadem attributed to the Empress Josephine

Diamonds and gold
H: 11.5 x W: 15 cm. (4½ x 5⅞")
Van Cleef & Arpels, New York

Traditionally attributed to the Empress Josephine, this
extraordinary gold diadem has 1,040 diamonds totaling
260 carats. It was a gift from Napoleon. After Josephine's
death, it was inherited by her daughter, Queen Hortense,
who left it to her son Napoleon III. His wife, the Empress
Eugénie, sold it after the fall of the Second Empire.

143 Empress Josephine

Henri-François Riesener (1767-1828)
Oil on canvas
H: 235 x L: 130 cm. (92½ x 51⅛″)
Signed and dated: 1806
Musée National du Château de Malmaison, N 3097
Given to the government by Prince and Princess Napoleon
  in payment of inheritance taxes, 1989

The son of the famous furniture-maker and the cousin
of Delacroix, Henri-François Riesener enjoyed a good
reputation as a portrait painter during the Empire and
the Restoration. This portrait of the Empress Josephine,
painted in 1806, was placed in the imperial palace in
Bordeaux where the Empress lived during the Spanish
crisis in 1808. Returned to the children of the Empress
during the Restoration, the picture remained in the
family's collections until recently. It has been restored
for this exhibition and is now on public display for the
first time.

144 Cameo-Shell Diadem of Josephine

Anonymous
Shell, gold, pearls, precious and semi-precious stones
H: 6.7 x L: 17 x W: 20 cm. (2⅝ x 6¾ x 7¾″)
Musée d'Art et d'Histoire, Palais Masséna, Nice, Inv. Chapsal 1163

This diadem was carved from a single shell and ornamented with gold,
pearls, and precious and semi-precious stones. It represents Apollo on
his chariot surrounded by the Four Seasons. It was given to Empress
Josephine by her brother-in-law Joachim Murat, King of Naples and
the husband of Caroline Bonaparte.

145 Queen Hortense

Jean-Baptiste, baron Regnault (1754-1829)
Oil on canvas (signed), circa 1810
H: 73 x L: 59.5 cm. (28¾ x 23⅜″)
Musée National du Château de Malmaison, MM 40-47-7232
Gift of Mrs. Helen Fahnestock-Hubbard, 1927

Hortense de Beauharnais, the daughter of the Empress
Josephine and of her first husband, Alexandre de
Beauharnais, was born in 1783. Her mother arranged
her marriage to Napoleon's brother Louis in 1802, and
the couple reigned over Holland from 1806 to 1810.
The marriage was unhappy, but it still produced three
sons, the youngest of whom was destined to become
Emperor of the French under the name of Napoleon III.
Exiled after Waterloo, Hortense died in Switzerland in
the small château of Arenenberg in 1837. As in the
portrait of her mother, Regnault here copied a part of
his large painting representing the marriage of Jerome
and Catherine de Württemberg (Château of Versailles).

146 Prince Eugène

Andrea Appiani (1754-1817)
Oil on canvas (signed and dated), 1810
H: 59 x L: 44 cm. (23¼ x 17⅜″)
Musée National du Château de Malmaison, MM 81-2-1
Gift of Charles-Otto Zieseniss, 1981

Eugène de Beauharnais, the son of the Empress
Josephine, was born in 1781. At a very young age, he
undertook a military career under the aegis of his step-
father Napoleon Bonaparte. Appointed Viceroy of Italy,
he reigned there from 1805 until 1814. He died in exile
in Munich in 1824. His marriage to the daughter of the
King of Bavaria produced several children, whose
descendants today reign as the Kings of Sweden,
Norway and Belgium, the Queens of Denmark and
Greece, and the Grand Duchess of Luxembourg.

147 **Marriage of Napoleon and Marie-Louise**

Georges Rouget (1784-1869)
Oil on canvas, 1810
H: 185 x L: 182 cm. (72 $^7/_8$ x 71 $^5/_8$″)
Signed and dated: GR 1810
Musée National du Château de Versailles, MV 1754

Since the Empress Josephine proved unable to give
Napoleon an heir, he married the daughter of the
Emperor of Austria, Archduchess Marie-Louise
(1791-1847). The civil ceremony was celebrated at
Saint Cloud on April 1. The next day, April 2, 1810, the
religious ceremony was held in the *Salon Carré* of the
Louvre, which had been transformed into a chapel for
the occasion. This is the scene which the artist represented
by copying the general composition of the large painting of the Coronation by his master, Jacques-Louis David.

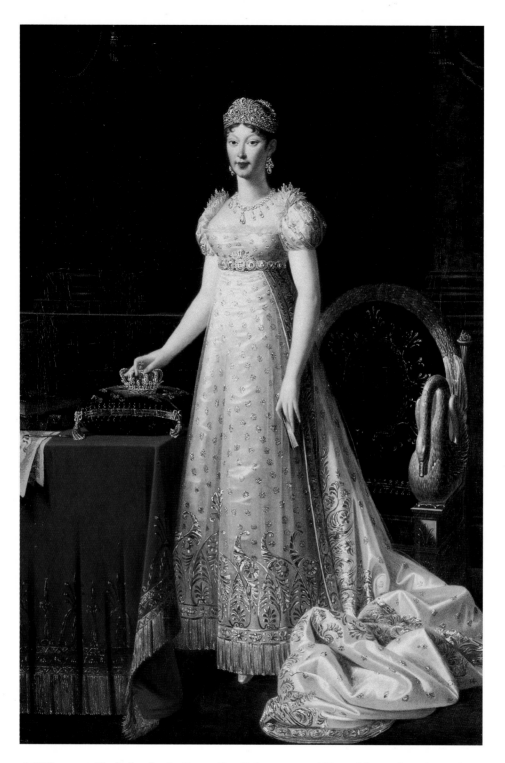

148 Empress Marie-Louise in Coronation Robes

Robert Lefèvre (1755-1830)
Oil on canvas (signed), 1812
H: 226 x L: 154.5 cm. (89 x 60 7/8")
Musée Chaumet, Paris

This official portrait of the new Empress was commissioned by the City of Metz in 1812, shortly after the birth of the King of Rome. Marie-Louise is shown wearing the diamond necklace which the Emperor had given her in honor of the birth of their son, and which is now in the collection of the Smithsonian Institution in Washington, D.C. The museums of Versailles and Parma have other copies of this portrait.

149 Necklace of Marie-Louise

François-Regnault Nitot
Diamonds, gold, 1811
L: 36 cm. (14 1/8")
Smithsonian Institution, Washington, D.C.
Gift of Mrs. Marjorie Merriweather Post, 1962

In 1811, Napoleon gave this sumptuous necklace (the same one shown in the portrait by Robert Lefèvre) to his wife to celebrate the birth of their son, the King of Rome. Marie-Louise took all her jewels with her in 1814 when she left France. When she died in 1847, she left them to her sister-in-law, Archduchess Sophie. The necklace remained in the Hapsburg family until it was sold in 1948 by Prince Franz Joseph of Lichtenstein. It belonged to several private owners before it was given to the Smithsonian by Mrs. Marjorie Merriweather Post.

150 Crown, Diadem, Comb, Necklace, Earrings and Bracelets of Marie-Louise

François-Regnault Nitot
Gold, white sapphires and garnets, 1811
Musée Chaumet, Paris

Several months after the wedding, François-Regnault Nitot made a set of ruby and diamond jewelry for the new Empress, including a crown, a diadem, a comb, a necklace, two earrings, two bracelets, and a belt. This extraordinary set is better known by this exact copy Nitot made for himself, substituting white sapphires for the diamonds and garnets for the rubies.

151 Diadem of Marie-Louise

François-Regnault Nitot
Diamonds, turquoise (formerly emeralds), gold, 1810
H: 8 x D: 16 cm. (3 ¹/₈ x 6¼″)
Smithsonian Institution, Washington, D.C.
Gift of Mrs. Marjorie Merriweather Post, 1973

In 1810, the Emperor commissioned a set of diamond and emerald jewelry from Nitot for his bride. The set included a necklace, a comb, and a diadem, which were to be the Empress' personal property. Marie-Louise took the jewels with her in 1814 when she left France. The set remained in the Hapsburg family until the twentieth century. The 79 emeralds in the diadem were unfortunately replaced by turquoise after 1953, although the piece still has all of its 1,068 diamonds.

152 Crown, Diadem, Comb, Necklace, Earrings and Bracelets of Marie-Louise

François-Regnault Nitot
Gouache
H: 102 x L: 82 cm. (40 ¹/₈ x 32¼″)
Musée Chaumet, Paris

The sketch shows the diamond and ruby jeweled belt as well.

153 **Marie-Louise and the King of Rome**

Jean-Baptiste Isabey (1767-1855)
Oil on vermeil
H: 29 x L: 25 x W: 5 cm. (11³⁄₈ x 9⁷⁄₈ x 2″)
Prince Napoleon, Paris, 551

This charming miniature was painted on a vermeil box
by Jean-Baptiste Isabey.

154 Napoleon's Gold *Nécessaire*

Martin-Guillaume Biennais (1764-1843)
Vermeil, crystal, porcelain, ivory, mother of pearl, steel,
  ebony, leather, mahogany, circa 1802
H: 52 x L: 36 x W: 18 cm. (20½ x 14 ⅛ x 7″)
Musée Carnavalet, Paris, OM608-610
Gift of General Bertrand, 1840

This is the most beautiful and largest of all the kits which Biennais made for Napoleon. It was delivered during the Consulate, then completed and repaired during the Empire with the ''B'' for Bonaparte being replaced by the Emperor's coat of arms in 1807. Among the 114 objects in the kit are a table service, toilet articles and practical instruments. Biennais subcontracted some of the pieces to the goldsmith François-Joseph Genu and others to Pierre-Nicolas Gamme. The Emperor considered it his most valuable kit, and he took it with him everywhere, even through all his battles. He reminisced on Saint Helena: ''My gold *nécessaire,* the one that served me the morning of the battles of Ulm, Austerlitz, Jena, Eylau, Friedland, the Isle of Lobeau, Moscow, and Montmirail, I want it to be precious for my son.'' Since he could no longer give it to the Duke of Reichstadt, General Bertrand donated it to the City of Paris in 1840.

155 Napoleon, Marie-Louise and the King of Rome in the Tuileries Gardens

Anonymous (attributed to Jacques-Louis David)
Oil on canvas
H: 53.5 x L: 45.5 cm. (21 x 17⁷/₈″)
Prince Napoleon, Paris, 11372

This work shows an unexpected side of the Emperor, walking in the gardens of the Tuileries Palace with his wife and son.

Madame de Montesquiou, the governess of the little king, ordered many toys for the boy. Although there was the usual baby's rattle, she preferred to buy him educational toys, which would either entertain him, like a wheelbarrow or this mallet, or prepare him for a military career, like a wooden rifle or this drum. Before his departure for Vienna in 1814, the little king gave this drum to the Emperor's official upholsterer, Delaitre, saying ''I cannot give you anything to remember me by, but here is my drum for your little boy.''

156 Drum of the King of Rome

Wood, copper, animal skin
H: 13 x D: 13 cm. (5¹/₈ x 5¹/₈″)
Musée National du Château de Fontainebleau, N 131
Acquired from Prince Napoleon, 1979

157 Mallet of the King of Rome

Boxwood, ebony, ivory
H: 21 x L: 6 cm. (8¼ x 2³/₈″)
Musée Carnavalet, Paris, OM 444
Gift Tinthouin, 1908

158 Rattle of the King of Rome

Vermeil and coral
H: 16 x L: 3.9 cm. (6³/₈ x 1½″)
Musée Carnavalet, Paris, OM 443
Gift Tinthouin, 1908

**159 The King of Rome
Seated on a Lamb**

Aimée Thibault (1780-1868)
Ink and wash
H: 20 x L: 24 cm. (7⅞ x 9½")
Prince Napoleon, Paris, 6582

Madame de Montesquiou commissioned this sketch
to give to the Emperor for his birthday on August 15,
1812. Napoleon was in Russia, and he did not receive
the gift until August 23, when he was at Smolensk.

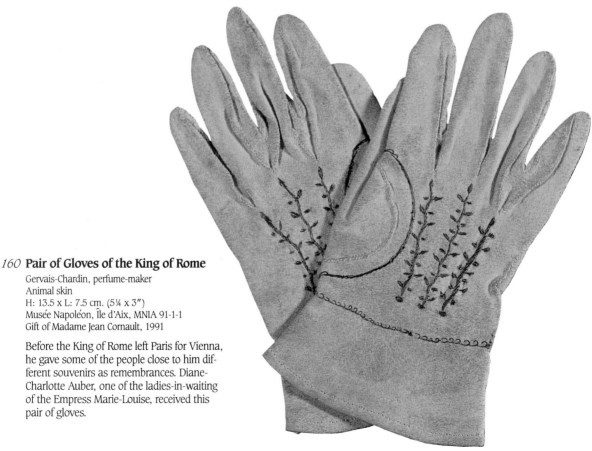

160 Pair of Gloves of the King of Rome

Gervais-Chardin, perfume-maker
Animal skin
H: 13.5 x L: 7.5 cm. (5¼ x 3")
Musée Napoléon, Île d'Aix, MNIA 91-1-1
Gift of Madame Jean Cornault, 1991

Before the King of Rome left Paris for Vienna,
he gave some of the people close to him different souvenirs as remembrances. Diane-
Charlotte Auber, one of the ladies-in-waiting
of the Empress Marie-Louise, received this
pair of gloves.

161 **Marie Walewska**

Robert Lefèvre (1755-1830)
Oil on canvas
H: 58.5 x D: 50.5 cm. (23 x 19 7/8″)
Private collection, Paris

The Emperor met the young Countess Walewska in
January 1807 near Warsaw. They immediately fell in
love, and their relationship lasted until Napoleon's exile.
After giving birth to the Emperor's son (Count Alexander
Walewski) in 1810, Marie settled in Paris and continued
to see Napoleon, who loved her dearly.

162 Wine Coolers for the Shah of Persia

163 Henry Auguste (died 1816)
Vermeil, enamel, 1809
H: 38.8 x L: 28 cm. (15¼ x 11″)
Signed: HY AUGUSTE FT A PARIS 1809
Prince Napoleon, Paris, 11476 and 11477

At the end of 1806, seeking to ally himself with Persia against Russia, Napoleon commissioned these two vases as a diplomatic present for the Shah of Persia, Feth-Ali. The wine coolers, which represent the two rulers, were not finished until 1809 and were never delivered to the Shah.

164 **Gold and Diamond Box
with a Portrait of the Emperor**

Etienne-Lucien Blerzy, master goldsmith (active 1798-circa
  1820), and Bernard-Amand Marguerite, jeweler
Gold, diamonds
H: 19 x L: 6 x W: 8.6 cm. (7½ x 2⅜ x 3⅜″)
Fondation Napoléon, Paris, Inv. bôite de présent 48
Former collection of Martial Lapeyre

The portrait of the Emperor is by Jean-Baptiste-Jacques
Augustin (1759-1832).

144

165 Gold, Diamond and Enamel Box with the Initial "L"

Jean-Louis Blerzy, master goldsmith
Gold, diamonds, blue enamel
H: 19 x L: 8.7 x W: 5.7 cm. (7½ x 3⅜ x 2¼″)
Fondation Napoléon, Paris, Inv. bôite de présent 08
Former collection of Martial Lapeyre

The initial "L" is that of Louis, King of Holland.

166 Gold and Enamel Box with the Initials "J.N."

Etienne-Lucien Blerzy, master goldsmith (active 1798-circa 1820), and Bernard-Amand Marguerite, jeweler
Gold, blue enamel
H: 19 x L: 9 x W: 5.9 cm. (7½ x 3½ x 2⅜″)
Fondation Napoléon, Paris, Inv. bôite de présent 01
Former collection of Martial Lapeyre

The initials "J.N." are those of Jerome-Napoléon, King of Westphalia.

167 Gold, Diamond and Enamel Box with the Initial "N"

Victorine Boizot
Gold, diamonds, blue enamel
H: 20 x L: 7.7 x W: 5.6 cm. (7⅞ x 3 x 2¼″)
Fondation Napoléon, Paris, Inv. bôite de présent 45
Former collection of Martial Lapeyre

The box has the initial of the Emperor Napoleon I.

168 Gold Box with the Initial "E"

Gabriel-Raoul Morel, master goldsmith (active 1798-1832)
Gold
H: 20 x L: 8.3 x W: 5.8 cm. (7⅞ x 3¼ x 2¼″)
Fondation Napoléon, Inv. bôite de présent 43
Former collection of Martial Lapeyre

The initial "E" is that of Prince Eugène de Beauharnais, Viceroy of Italy. The box was given by him to Baron Larrey, the surgeon of Napoleon's Grand Army.

169 *Redingote* (Greatcoat) of Napoleon

Chevallier, tailor
Fabric
H: 132.5 x L: 30.5 cm. (52⅛ x 12″)
Musée National du Château de Fontainebleau, Paris, N 264
Gift of Prince Napoleon and Countess de Witt

Napoleon's famous grey *redingote* was simply the overcoat that infantry officers wore during the *Ancien Régime*. Six of these overcoats were in the Emperor's wardrobe, some of which were green, and some blue. Napoleon took three to Saint Helena with him, two grey coats and one green. All three are now in the collection of the Château of Fontainebleau. The Emperor willed this one to his son, the Duke of Reichstadt.

170 Napoleon's Campaign Tent

Poussin and Lejeune
Brussels duck, toile de Jouy, wool
H: 435 x L: 667 x W: 328 cm.
 (14' 2¼" x 21' 7³⁄₈" x 10' 6³⁄₈")
Mobilier National, Paris, GMT 2462

This oval tent with two poles is one of the models
delivered to Napoleon's army in 1808 for the Spanish
Campaign. The Emperor's tent had two rooms—a work
space with folding chairs and tables, and a bedroom
with the famous folding iron bed. The ground was
covered with a wool rug in a leopard-skin pattern.

Napoleonic Campaign Furniture

This campaign furniture, most often made by Jacob-Desmalter, followed
Napoleon in his campaigns throughout Europe. Easy to transport, the
folding campstools, chairs and tables could be hooked together once they
had been set up so that the Emperor could spread out his maps.

171 Folding Campstools

Ash, iron, canvas, wool, green hide
H: 45 x L: 49 x W: 48 cm. (17¾ x 19¼ x 18⁷⁄₈")
Mobilier National, Paris, GMT 2424

172 Folding Chairs

Beech, iron, canvas, wool, green hide
H: 87 x L: 41 x W: 40 cm. (34¼ x 16¹⁄₈ x 15¾")
Mobilier National, Paris, GMT 2427

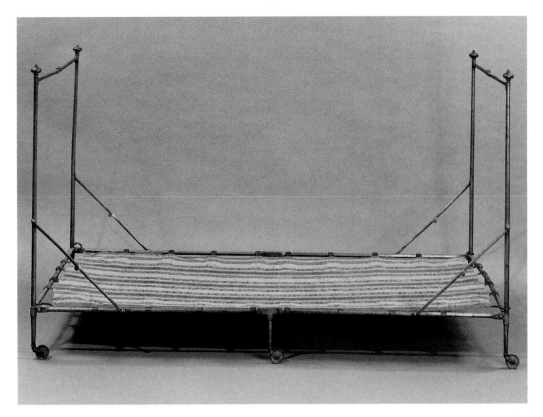

173 **Napoleon's Campaign Bed**

Desouches
Iron, copper, canvas
H: 108 x L: 182 x W: 86 cm. (42½ x 71⅝ x 33⅞″)
Musée National du Château de Malmaison, MM 40-47-2994
Gift of Mr. and Mrs. Edward Tuck, 1911

Napoleon adopted this type of folding bed during the Consulate. There were several models, like this one, which could be transported on the back of a mule, and other, bigger models which were put on wagons. They were all made by the locksmith Desouches. General Bertrand brought this bed back from Saint Helena.

174 **Folding Tables**

Poplar, walnut, iron
H: 70 x L: 74 x W: 47 cm. (27½ x 26⅛ x 18½″)
Mobilier National, Paris, GMT 952

175 Napoleon's Breastplate

Steel, gold, velvet
H: 44 x D: 92 cm. (17 3/8 x 36¼")
Musée National de la Légion d'Honneur et des
  Ordres de Chevalerie, Paris, 05884
Gift of Prince de la Tour d'Auvergne-Lauraguais

Napoleon thought it would be prudent to require his
generals and commanding officers to wear a breastplate on the battlefield. To set the example, he had one
made for himself and another for Maréchal Berthier.
This breastplate was delivered in 1807. The Emperor
wore it during the Battle of Tilsit, but found it so
uncomfortable that he abandoned his idea.

176 Napoleon's Helmet

Steel, gold, leather, horsehair, 1807
H: 110 x L: 21 x W: 40 cm. (43¼ x 8¼ x 15¾")
Musée National de la Legion d'Honneur et des
  Ordres de Chevalerie, Paris, 05885
Gift of Prince de la Tour d'Auvergne-Lauraguais

177 Napoleon's Hunting Rifle

Jean-Adrien-Prosper Lepage
Walnut, leather, silver, gold
L: 133 cm. (52 3/8")
Signed: LE PAGE A PARIS ARQUEBUSIER DE L'EMPEREUR
Fondation Napoléon, Paris, Inv. militaria et
  souvenirs historiques 03
Former collection Martial Lapeyre

Of all the Emperor's remaining rifles, this one offers the
greatest historical significance. It has a silver medallion
which is engraved with the following phrase: *"Île d'Aix
le 15 juillet à 8 heures du soir 1815* (Île d'Aix , July 15,
8 p.m., 1815).'' Napoleon gave this rifle to the navy
lieutenant Jean-Victor Besson who had concocted a
plan whereby Napoleon could escape from the Ile d'Aix
to the United States. The plan had first been adopted,
then refused by Napoleon, who finally decided to surrender to the English. Thanking his loyal follower for
the help he had given him, the Emperor said to Besson:
''I have nothing left in this world to give you, my
friend, other than this rifle. Please take it to
remember me by.''

178 Napoleon's Campaign Map of Germany

Chauchard and Dezauche
Paper glued to canvas, 1801
H: 180 x L: 253 cm. (70⅞ x 99⅝″) unfolded
Musée de l'Armée, Paris, Ed 96

The Emperor relied on this map of Germany during the campaign of 1813.

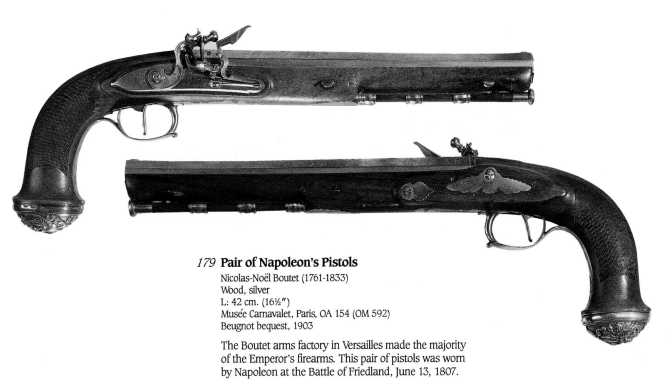

179 Pair of Napoleon's Pistols

Nicolas-Noël Boutet (1761-1833)
Wood, silver
L: 42 cm. (16½″)
Musée Carnavalet, Paris, OA 154 (OM 592)
Beugnot bequest, 1903

The Boutet arms factory in Versailles made the majority of the Emperor's firearms. This pair of pistols was worn by Napoleon at the Battle of Friedland, June 13, 1807.

180

181

182

La Grande Armée

The Empire's Great Army was one of Napoleon's most remarkable achievements. This finely honed, powerful instrument was everything a sovereign could hope for. The idea first took shape in the army which was victorious at Marengo. From 1805 to 1809, the number of troops rose regularly. 73,000 men fought in the Austerlitz campaign and on the Jena battlefield, while there were 187,000 at Wagram. The numbers then declined—125,000 in the battle of Moscow, 100,000 in Dresden, and 135,000 in Leipzig. By 1814, the total had dwindled to an average of 30,000 men during the skirmishes in France. At Waterloo, however, Napoleon succeeded in mobilizing the same number of men as at Austerlitz.

The Emperor was very attentive to the morale of his soldiers, and constantly reminded them of France's great destiny. The uniforms worn at headquarters or on the battlefield were very different from parade uniforms or even the uniforms worn for major battles like those of Austerlitz or Moscow. On these occasions, each regiment tried to outdo the others by the cut and decoration of uniforms. The eagle standard which the Emperor personally presented to the regiments became the object of a veritable cult among the soldiers.

In the final analysis, the Great Army, although ultimately vanquished at Waterloo, had numerous victories to its credit, and its final defeat did not reduce its stature as one of history's major military formations.

Raoul Brunon, Curator
Musée de l'Empéri, Salon-de-Provence

180 Brigadier General's Uniform, Light Cavalry

H: 180 x L: 60 x W: 60 cm. (70 7/8 x 23 5/8 x 23 5/8")
Musée de l'Empéri (Musée de l'Armée), Salon-de-Provence
Former collection Raoul and Jean Brunon

Empire generals and marshals sometimes added their own flourishes to their uniforms. The uniforms of the light cavalry were particularly elaborate, styled *à la hongroise* (in the Hungarian fashion). Generals wore their stars on the sleeves of their jackets.

181 Officer's Uniform, *Chasseurs à pied* of the Imperial Guard

H: 210 x L: 70 x W: 60 cm. (82 5/8 x 27 1/2 x 23 5/8")
Musée de l'Empéri (Musée de l'Armée), Salon-de-Provence
Former collection Raoul and Jean Brunon

The Imperial Guard, which was made up of the bravest, most handsome soldiers, constituted the elite of Napoleon's Great Army. It was a formation on which the Emperor knew he could count in all circumstances. The *Chasseurs à pied* and the *Grenadiers à pied,* which could be recognized by their famous bear-skin busbies, formed the infantry divisions of the elite ''Old Guard.''

182 Infantryman's Uniform with an Eagle Standard

H: 220 x L: 70 x W: 140 cm. (86 5/8 x 27 1/2 x 55 1/8")
Musée de l'Empéri (Musée de l'Armée), Salon-de-Provence
Former collection Raoul and Jean Brunon

Although it was the army's most difficult job, the infantry was one of the pillars of the Great Army. Carrying his long rifle with the bayonet attached and with his cowskin knapsack and rolled overcoat on his back, the Napoleonic foot-soldier traipsed across Europe, from the Spanish Sierras to the steppes of Russia.

183 Dragoon's Uniform

H: 200 x L: 70 x W: 60 cm. (78¾ x 27½ x 23⅝")
Musée de l'Empéri (Musée de l'Armée), Salon-de-Provence
Former collection Raoul and Jean Brunon

The Dragoons had many responsibilities, either fighting on horseback or sometimes in light cavalry divisions as foot-soldiers. The Dragoons wore an old-fashioned helmet, similar to that of the *Cuirassiers*, but it was made of copper and decorated with the skin of a panther or a seal. Like the battle cavalry, they wore leather breeches.

184 Twelfth Regiment Hussard's Uniform

H: 190 x L: 60 x W: 60 cm. (74¾ x 23⅝ x 23⅝")
Musée de l'Empéri (Musée de l'Armée), Salon-de-Provence
Former collection Raoul and Jean Brunon

The Hussards and the *Chasseurs à cheval* made up the light cavalry divisions in charge of reconnaissance. Their mission was also the pursuit and harassment of the enemy which required much initiative, endurance and daring. The Hussards, with their uniforms *à la hongroise* (in the Hungarian fashion), were some of the most striking horsemen in the army. Each of the fourteen regiments had its own color.

185 *Carabinier-Cuirassier's* Uniform

H: 210 x L: 60 x W: 60 cm. (82⅝ x 23⅝ x 23⅝")
Musée de l'Empéri (Musée de l'Armée), Salon-de-Provence
Former collection Raoul and Jean Brunon

The *Carabiniers* were an elite unit of the *Cuirassiers*. On the battlefield, these cavalry formations were especially trained to charge the enemy and to guarantee victory in the most crucial moments of battle. Fifteen thousand *Carabiniers* and *Cuirassiers* participated in the Russian Campaign. ''It is difficult to imagine the impression our reserve of *Cuirassiers* made; it was like a wall of iron. The *Carabiniers* were even more amazing—they looked like giant horsemen from the Middle Ages.''

186 Eagle from an Eagle Standard

Pierre-Philippe Thomire, (1751-1843), after Antoine-Denis
  Chaudet (1763-1810)
H: 23 x W: 23 cm. (9 x 9″)
Musée de l'Empéri (Musée de l'Armée), Salon-de-Provence
Former collection Raoul and Jean Brunon

Napoleon personally chose the spread-winged eagle
as the emblem of the Empire. His selection was inspired
by the Roman eagle of Antiquity, a symbol of power
and courage. Thus, the insignia of each regiment
came to be known as an ''eagle.''

Crafted by some of the period's best artists in gilt
bronze, the eagle was mounted on a standard. There,
the Emperor's dedication was written in gold letters,
e.g. ''The Emperor of the French to the First Infantry
Regiment.''

187 Medallion of Prince Murat

After Lorenzo Bartolini (1777-1830)
Marble
D: 34 cm. (13⅜")
Bibliothèque Marmottan, Boulogne-Billancourt, Inv. 70-364
Gift of Paul Marmottan

Murat was the best cavalry officer of his time, and his legendary charges enabled Napoleon to win many battles.

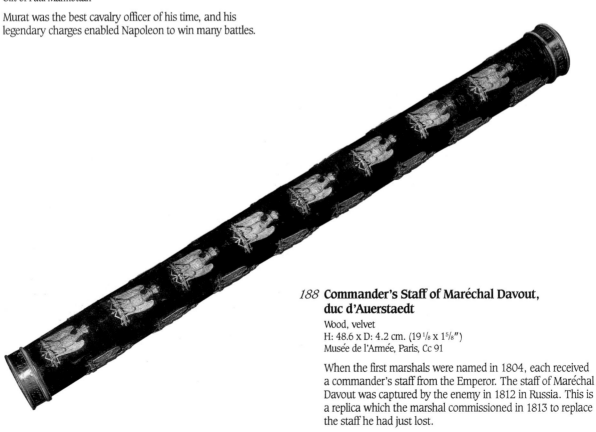

**188 Commander's Staff of Maréchal Davout,
duc d'Auerstaedt**

Wood, velvet
H: 48.6 x D: 4.2 cm. (19⅛ x 1⅝")
Musée de l'Armée, Paris, Cc 91

When the first marshals were named in 1804, each received a commander's staff from the Emperor. The staff of Maréchal Davout was captured by the enemy in 1812 in Russia. This is a replica which the marshal commissioned in 1813 to replace the staff he had just lost.

189 Napoleon Seated Consulting a Map

Charles-Stanilas Canlers (died 1812), after Antoine Mouton,
  called Moutoni (1765–after 1827)
Gilt bronze, sea-green marble, 1809
H: 44 x L: 29 x W: 29 cm. (17¼ x 11⅜ x 11⅜″)
Private collection, Paris

Commissioned in 1807, the statuette of *Napoleon
Seated Consulting a Map* was not finished by
Moutoni until 1809. Six copies were made by
Canlers—four in bronze and two in silver. This
is the only copy known to exist in gilt bronze.

190 Sketch of the Arc of Triumph

Anonymous
Ink wash on paper
H: 44 x L: 59.5 cm. (17⅜ x 23⅜")
Archives Nationales, Paris, N III Seine 1164, pièce 4

In order to close the perspective at the end of the Tuileries Gardens, the Emperor decided to build a triumphal arch in memory of his armies on the hilltop called *l'Etoile*. The cornerstone was laid in 1806, and the blueprints of the architect Jean-François-Thérèse Chalgrin (1739-1811) were adopted. When the Empire fell, the monument was only about 65 feet high. It was not completed until 1836 under the reign of Louis-Philippe.

192

191 The Day after the Battle of Eylau

Charles Meynier (1768-1832)
Oil on canvas
H: 93 x L: 146 cm. (36⅝ x 57½")
Musée National du Château de Versailles, MV 8128
Purchase, 1960

Prussia, which alone resisted the French Empire, was defeated at Jena in 1806.
The following year, the Russians met the French in battle at Eylau, then at Friedland,
before agreeing to negotiate at Tilsit. Both armies were decimated in the Battle of
Eylau, on February 8, 1807, and although the French were victors on the battlefield,
15,000 soldiers died and 20,000 were wounded.

192 Napoleon Visiting the Bivouacs on the Eve of the Battle of Austerlitz

Louis Bacler d'Albe (1761-1848)
Oil on canvas (signed)
H: 290 x L: 228 cm. (114⅛ x 89¾")
Musée National du Château de Versailles, MV 1710
Salon of 1808

Exactly one year after the Coronation, on December 2, 1805,
Napoleon fought his fortieth battle against the third Austrian-
Russian coalition, which he crushed at Austerlitz. On the eve
of the battle, the Emperor paid a visit to the troops who set
bails of hay on fire as an honor guard. The enemy mistakenly
thought that the French had burned their bivouacs and were
planning to retreat.

193 **Napoleon's Bivouac on the Battlefield of Wagram, Night of July 5-6, 1809**

Adolphe-Eugène Roehn (1780-1867)
Oil on canvas
H: 229 x L: 228 cm. (90⅛ x 89¾")
Musée National du Château de Versailles, MV 1744
Salon of 1810

During the spring of 1809, the Austrians invaded Bavaria, and Napoleon was obliged to take up
arms once again. He pushed back the Austrians and then dealt them a decisive blow in the Battle
of Wagram. This victory reduced Austria to a second-rate power, and the Emperor Francis had no
choice but to give his daughter, Marie-Louise, to Napoleon in marriage.

194 The Crossing of the Avis Pass

Louis-François, baron Lejeune (1775-1848)
Oil on canvas, 1817
H: 210 x L: 260 cm. (82 5/8 x 102 3/8″)
Purchase, 1861

In 1808, ignoring Spanish protests, Napoleon named his brother Joseph King of Spain. Joseph's adopted country fought against the French for five long years, and Napoleon's best soldiers were hard pressed to eliminate Spanish resistance. The guerrilla warfare took its toll, such as when the Spanish opened fire on the French just as they had entered the Avis Pass on April 11, 1811.

195 Carriage Used by Napoleon in the Russian Campaign

Getting, carriagemaker
Wood, leather, iron, fabric
H: 233 x L: 409 x W: 256 cm. (7' 5³/₈" x 13' 3³/₈" x 8' 3¼")
Musée National du Château de Malmaison, MM 75-12-1
Gift of Count Blücher von Wahlstatt, 1975

This carriage, ordered in 1812 for the Russian Campaign, was not delivered until the Emperor was already at Vilna, because the carriagemaker had so much work in preparation for the campaign. It was a new model which could be closed if the weather was inclement, or opened if the Emperor wanted to ride through the ranks during the battle and issue last minute orders. The carriage was used during the whole Russian Campaign, but was captured by the Prussians after the Battle of Waterloo in Genappe on June 18, 1815. It was presented to Marshal Blücher and remained in his family. It is the only carriage that still has its original decoration with the Empire coat of arms.

196 Battle of Polotsk, August 18, 1812

Jean-Charles Langlois (1789-1870)
Oil on canvas
H: 233 x L: 256 cm. (91¾ x 100¾″)
Signed and dated: C. LANGLOIS 1838
Musée National du Château de Versailles, MV 1761
Commissioned by Louis-Philippe, 1836

In June 1812, Napoleon's troops crossed the Niemen River without declaring war. The victories of Smolensk and Borodino cleared the way to Moscow; however, the burning of Moscow and the approaching winter obliged the Emperor to retreat. The Russian winter, in fact, decimated the Great Army, which had lost hundreds of thousands of soldiers by the end of 1812.

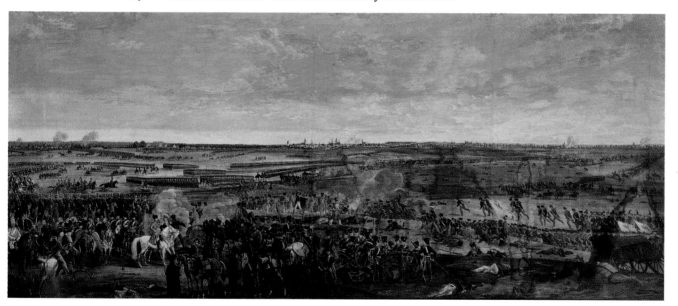

197 Napoleon at the Battle of Leipzig

Anonymous
Gouache on canvas
H: 120 x L: 250 cm. (47¼ x 98½″)
Bibliothèque Marmottan, Boulogne-Billancourt, Inv. 70-193
Gift of Paul Marmottan

Also shown page 39

Once the Great Army had been defeated, the people of Europe united to fight against further French domination. In the Battle of Leipzig on October 13, 1813, more than 100,000 men were killed or wounded, as the French army was beaten by the allied powers—the Prussians, Russians, English and Austrians. It was the beginning of the end.

198 Russian Prisoners Marching down the Boulevard Saint-Martin after the Battle of Montmirail, February 17, 1814

Etienne-Jean Delécluze (1781-1863)
Watercolor
H: 35 x L: 65 cm. (13¾ x 25½")
Signed and dated: VIDIT ET DELINEAVIT E.J. DELECLUZE 1814
Musée National du Château de Versailles, MV 5193
Gift of Etienne-Jean Delécluze, 1862

Shown also page 39

199 Wounded French Soldiers Returning to Paris, Marching down the Boulevard Saint-Martin after the Battle of Montmirail, February 17, 1814

Etienne-Jean Delécluze (1781-1863)
Watercolor
H: 35 x L: 104 cm. (13¾ x 41")
Signed and dated: E.J. DELECLUZE VIDIT ET DELINEAVIT 1814
Musée National du Château de Versailles, MV 5194
Gift of Etienne-Jean Delécluze, 1862

200 The Allied Attack on Paris

Bernardini
Watercolor and gouache on paper
H: 52 x L: 87 cm. (20½ x 34¼")
Musée de L'Île de France, Sceaux, Inv. 37.2.4

On March 30, 1814, Blücher's right flank moved onto
the hill at Montmartre, from which the allies were able
to bomb Paris with no interference. After having had no
success in stopping the enemy, Maréchal Marmont surrendered Paris, since no further resistance was possible.

201 Napoleon Bids Farewell to His Generals at Fontainebleau

Jean-Pierre-Marie Jazet (1788-1871),
 after Horace Vernet (1789-1863)
Engraving
H: 88 x L: 103 cm. (34⅝ x 40½")
Musée National du Château de Malmaison
 MM 40-47-8131
Gift of Prince George of Greece, 1958

Once Paris had surrendered, the Emperor
was pressed by his marshals to offer no further
resistance. He resigned himself to this state of
affairs and abdicated at Fontainebleau on April
6, 1814. On April 20, he bid farewell to the
Imperial Guard in the courtyard of the Château
of Fontainebleau before leaving for Elba.

202 **The Battle of Waterloo**

Henri-Félix-Emmanuel Philippoteaux (1815-1884)
Oil on canvas, 1874
H: 159 x W: 215 cm. (62⁵/₈ x 84⁵/₈″)
Wellington Museum, Apsley House, London

At Waterloo, Napoleon had only 124,000 men to fight the coalition army made up of Wellington's
95,000 English and Dutch soldiers and Blücher's 124,000 Prussians. On June 18, 1815, although
they defended themselves heroically, the French were defeated, and then pursued by Blücher.
Amidst the general rout, only the legendary Old Guard retreated in formation.

203 Portrait of the Duke of Wellington

Sir Thomas Lawrence (1769-1830)
Oil on canvas
H: 107 x W: 86 cm. (42 1/8 x 33 7/8")
Wellington Museum, Apsley House, London

Arthur Wellesley, Duke of Wellington (1769-1852), had already fought against Napoleon's armies when he commanded the British troops in Spain. He defeated the French at Vitoria (1813) and then invaded the south of France, pushing onto Toulouse (1814). As commander of the allied forces, he won a decisive victory over Napoleon at Waterloo on June 18, 1815. He then commanded the occupation forces in France until 1818.

204 Portrait of Field Marshal Prince von Blücher

Sir Thomas Lawrence (1769-1830)
Oil on canvas
H: 88 x W: 73 cm. (34 5/8 x 28¾")
Wellington Museum, Apsley House, London

Gebhard-Lebrecht von Blücher (1742-1819) entered Paris in 1814 with the allied troops. Named commander of the Prussian army the following year, he was first defeated by Napoleon at Ligny on June 16, 1815, before joining up with Wellington at Waterloo on June 18 to participate in the French army's final defeat.

205 Soldier's Breastplate from the Battle of Waterloo

Steel
H: 38 x L: 34.4 x W: 30 cm. (15 x 13½ x 11¾")
Musée de l'Armée, Paris, Cc 206

Found on the battlefield at Waterloo, this breastplate belonged to François-Antoine Fauveau (1792-1815), a former butter dealer, who was exceptionally tall for the period—almost 5'9."

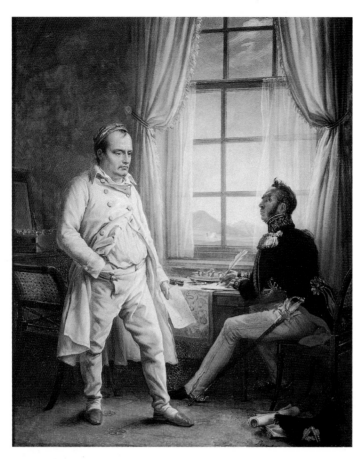

206 Napoleon Dictating His Memoirs to General Gourgaud

Karl-August von Steuben (1788-1856)
Oil on canvas
H: 65 x L: 55 cm. (25⅝ x 21⅝″)
Private collection, Paris

Shown also page 43

General Gaspard Gourgaud (1783-1852), Napoleon's aide-de-camp, followed the Emperor to Saint Helena. Napoleon dictated his recollections to Gourgaud, intending to use them later to write his autobiography. Gourgaud returned to Europe in 1818 and published his memoirs, which, together with those of Las Cases, Montholon and Bertrand, give a graphic picture of the life of the illustrious exile.

207 Longwood on Saint Helena

Louis-Joseph-Narcisse, comte Marchand (1791-1876)
Watercolor, gouache, 1821
H: 33 x L: 47 cm. (13 x 18½″)
Bibliothèque Marmottan, Boulogne-Billancourt, Inv. 70-134
Gift of Paul Marmottan

This moving scene was painted shortly after the death of the Emperor by his valet, Count Marchand. With the Tuileries Palace, Longwood holds the record for being the residence Napoleon lived in longest.

Longwood was a rather small house situated on a wind-swept plain. It was used as a summer residence before the Emperor came to live on Saint Helena. The English built several additions to house Napoleon's staff and servants. About thirty people lived in close quarters in these buildings around a small garden planted in 1819. This modest building was bought by Napoleon III in 1858 and now belongs to the French government which administers this remote site.

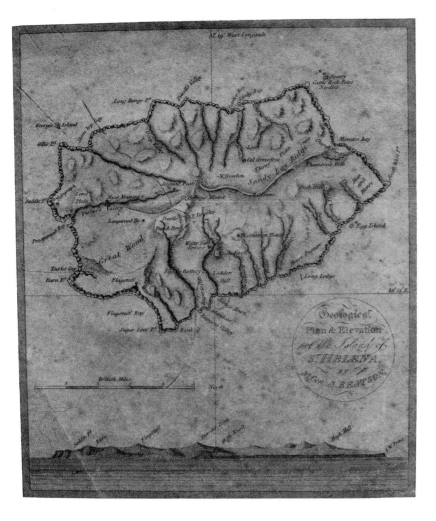

208 Map of Saint Helena Annotated by Napoleon

Paper
H: 27.5 x L: 22 cm. (10⁷/₈ x 8⁵/₈″)
Musée de Sens

209 Eagle from Napoleon's Silver Service

Martin-Guillaume Biennais (1764-1843)
Silver, marble
H: 22.5 cm. (8⁷/₈″)
Prince Napoleon, Paris, 241

This eagle decorated one of the large pieces of silver used
by Napoleon on Saint Helena. The English governor,
Sir Hudson Lowe, imposed restrictions on expenses;
thus, the Emperor decided in 1816 to have his silver
service melted down and sold. He kept several of the
eagles, which he willed to various members of the
Bonaparte family.

210 **Napoleon's Clock from Saint-Helena**

Gilt bronze
H: 45 x L: 36 x W: 14 cm. (17¾ x 14 ⅛ x 5½")
Prince Napoleon, Paris, 219

This clock, called the rose clock, was taken to Saint
Helena by Madame de Montholon. She gave it to
the Emperor who used it in his bedroom.

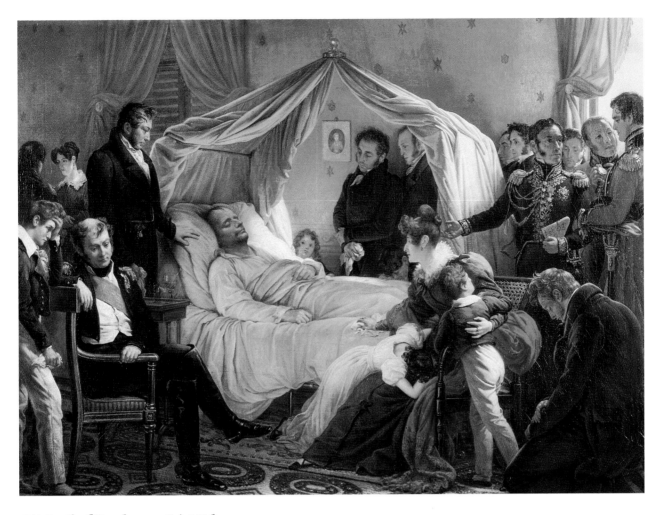

211 Death of Napoleon on Saint Helena

Karl-August von Steuben (1788-1856)
Oil on canvas, circa 1828
H: 89 x L: 115 cm. (35 x 45¼")
Napoleonmuseum, Arenenberg, Switzerland, Inv. 1978/6

Napoleon had stomach cancer, which began to develop rapidly towards the end of 1820. In the spring of 1821, his doctors, Arnott and Antommarchi, visited him every day, but they were unable to stop the progression of the disease. The Emperor had great difficulty retaining the food he ate. He died on May 5, 1821, at 5:49 p.m., giving up what Chateaubriand called ''the most powerful breath of life as ever animated human clay.''

212 Napoleon's Death Mask

Attributed to Francesco Antommarchi (1789-1838)
Plaster
H: 35 x L: 30 cm. (13¾ x 11¾")
Musée National du Château de Malmaison,
  MM 40-47-7284
Purchase, 1944

Two days after the Emperor's death, Dr. Burton, assisted by Antommarchi, made a three-piece death mask of the Emperor's face. Aided and abetted by Countess Bertrand, Antommarchi took the central piece and reconstituted the missing parts. He rapidly made several plaster casts which he gave to those close to the Emperor, before commercializing hundreds of copies, which were sold to the public by subscription. This death mask is Antommarchi's personal copy, which remained in his family until 1944.

213

214

213 Napoleon I

Charles-Marie-Emile Seurre (1798-1858)
Bronze
H: 190.5 x D: 56 cm. (75 x 22″)
Signed: E. SEURRE, SCULPTEUR; SOYER ET INGER, FONDEURS
Musée National du Château de Versailles, MV 1520
Purchased by Louis-Philippe from the artist in 1834 for
the galleries of the Château de Versailles

This life-size statue is the reduction of a monumental work which
was placed on the top of the Vendôme Column in 1833 by order of
Louis-Philippe. It was installed in the courtyard of the Invalides in
1911. It replaced the statue of Napoleon as a Roman emperor which
had been on top of the column during the Empire and was melted
down when the Bourbons returned to power. The Emperor is shown
here in a familiar pose as the legendary "little Corporal," with his
black hat and grey *redingote.*

214 Model of the Vendôme Column

Nicolas-Guy-Antoine Brenet (1770-1846)
Bronze, circa 1832
H: 184 x L: 25 cm. (72½ x 9⅞″)
Direction des Monnaies et Médailles, Musée de la Monnaie,
Paris, Inv. 230

The medal-maker Brenet made several copies (scale 1/24) of the model of the Vendôme
Column he had presented in the Salon of 1834. At that time, the monumental statue of
Seurre, now in the courtyard of the Invalides, was on the top of the column. The real
name of the monument was the Column of the Great Army, or the Austerlitz Column.
Designed by the architect Jean-Baptiste Lepère (1761-1844), it was begun in 1806 and
finished in 1810. A statue by Chaudet representing Napoleon as a Roman emperor was
put on top. The bronze used to cast it came from cannons captured from the Austrians
during the campaign of 1805.

215 Life of Napoleon in Eight Hats

Karl-August von Steuben (1788-1856)
Oil on canvas, 1826
H: 26 x L: 29 cm. (10¼ x 11⅜″)
Musée National du Château de Malmaison, MM 85-3-1
Purchase, 1985

Only after Louis-Philippe came to power in 1830 could
Napoleonic scenes be freely represented. When it was
painted in 1826, this painting was simply called *Story
of a Hat,* to keep the artist from getting into trouble
with the Bourbon authorities. The eight hats illustrate
the rise and fall of the Emperor, with an eagle, the towers
of Notre-Dame Cathedral, the Moscow fire, and Saint
Helena in the background.

Though in his will Napoleon asked that his ashes be scattered "on the banks of the Seine, among the French people I have loved so much," he was initially buried on St. Helena, the despised island of his imprisonment. In 1833, French King Louis-Philippe initiated negotiations with the British government for the return of Napoleon's body. Finally, after seven years of often-frustrating deliberations, Britain agreed to release Napoleon's body to France.

King Louis-Philippe immediately dispatched his son, the Prince of Joinville, to collect the Emperor's remains. Upon his arrival, the coffin was exhumed and briefly opened to ensure authenticity. The body of the Emperor who had been dead for nineteen years had remained in a state of perfect preservation.

The remains were returned to Paris amid great fanfare. Crowds braved the brutal winter weather in order to catch a glimpse of their beloved Emperor's coffin. While a tomb befitting the Emperor was created, his coffin remained in St. Jerome's cathedral. Napoleon's body was laid to final rest in the Hôtel des Invalides (Home for Disabled Soldiers) on April 3, 1861.

The grandeur of the tomb reflects the splendor and greatness Napoleon sought during his lifetime. The Emperor's sarcophagus dominates its circular crypt which is flanked by twelve colossal statues celebrating Napoleon's great battles. Low reliefs around the gallery depict institutions founded by the Emperor. Nearby, resides the coffin of the King of Rome, Napoleon's cherished son.

Comparing Countries

Games and Entertainment

Compara países

Juegos y ocio

translated into Spanish by María P Coira

Sabrina Crewe

CRABTREE
PUBLISHING COMPANY
WWW.CRABTREEBOOKS.COM

CRABTREE
PUBLISHING COMPANY
WWW.CRABTREEBOOKS.COM

Author: Sabrina Crewe

Editorial director: Kathy Middleton

Designer: Keith Williams

Illustrator: Stefan Chabluk

Translator: María P Coira

Proofreader: Crystal Sikkens

Production coordinator and prepress: Ken Wright

Print coordinator: Katherine Berti

Every attempt has been made to clear copyright.
Should there be any inadvertent omission please
apply to the publisher for rectification.

The publisher would like to thank the following for permission
to reproduce their pictures: Igor Bulgarin/Shutterstock 5; Cdrin/
Shutterstock 14; Eric Chretien/Gamma-Rapho/Getty Images 28;
Deutsches Museum 27; Johannes Eisele/AFP/Getty Images 12;
Tristan Fewings/Getty Images 18; Greatstock/Alamy Stock Photo 9;
Victor Jiang/Shutterstock 29; Bundit Jonwise/Shutterstock title page;
Denis Kabelev/Shutterstock 7; Richard Paul Kane/Shutterstock 15;
Kamira/Shutterstock 21; Katacarix/Shutterstock 10; Patryk Kosmider/
Shutterstock 22; Lazyllama/Shutterstock 8; Tony Magdaraog/
Shutterstock 25; Manfredxy/Shutterstock front cover (bottom);
Mauritius Images GmbH/Alamy Stock Photo 6; Nila Newsom/
Shutterstock 23; Ron Nickel/Getty Images 4; Giannis Papanikos/
Shutterstock 19; PCN Photography/Alamy Stock Photo 13; Tatiana
Popova/Shutterstock 7 (inset); Premier Photo/Shutterstock 26;
Galina Savina/Shutterstock 17; Stephan/Wikimedia Commons 16;
Stiop/Shutterstock 11; Suchan/Shutterstock 24; Masa Uemura/Alamy
Stock Photo 20; Ververidis Vasilis/Shutterstock front cover (top).

Library and Archives Canada Cataloguing in Publication

Title: Games and entertainment = Juegos y ocio / Sabrina Crewe.
Other titles: Juegos y ocio
Names: Crewe, Sabrina, author. | Coira, María P., translator.
Description: Series statement: Comparing countries = Compara países |
    Translated into Spanish by María P. Coira. |
    Previously published: London: Franklin Watts, 2018. | Includes index. |
    Text in English and Spanish.
Identifiers: Canadiana (print) 20190199180 |
    Canadiana (ebook) 20190199199 |
    ISBN 9780778769415 (hardcover) |
    ISBN 9780778769620 (softcover) |
    ISBN 9781427124418 (HTML)
Subjects: LCSH: Games—Juvenile literature. | LCSH: Amusements—
    Juvenile literature. | LCSH: Play—Juvenile literature.
Classification: LCC GV1203 .C74 2020 | DDC j306.4/8—dc23

Library of Congress Cataloging-in-Publication Data

Names: Crewe, Sabrina, author. | Crewe, Sabrina. Games and
    entertainment. | Crewe, Sabrina. Games and entertainment. Spanish
Title: Games and entertainment = Juegos y ocio / Sabrina Crewe.
Other titles: Juegos y ocio
Description: New York, New York : Crabtree Publishing Company, 2020.
    | Series: Comparing countries | Includes index.
Identifiers: LCCN 2019043503 (print) | LCCN 2019043504 (ebook) |
    ISBN 9780778769415 (hardcover) |
    ISBN 9780778769620 (paperback) |
    ISBN 9781427124418 (ebook)
Subjects: LCSH: Games--Juvenile literature.
Classification: LCC GV1203 .C75 2020 (print) | LCC GV1203 (ebook) |
    DDC 790.1/922--dc23
LC record available at https://lccn.loc.gov/2019043503
LC ebook record available at https://lccn.loc.gov/2019043504

Crabtree Publishing Company
www.crabtreebooks.com   1-800-387-7650

Published in 2020 by Crabtree Publishing Company

Published in Canada
Crabtree Publishing
616 Welland Avenue
St. Catharines, ON
L2M 5V6

Published in the United States
Crabtree Publishing
PMB 59051
350 Fifth Ave, 59th Floor
New York, NY 10118

Printed in the U.S.A./012020/CG20191115

Contents

Fun around the world · 4

Board games and cards · 6

Children's games · 8

Races and competitions · 10

Olympic Games · 12

Football and soccer · 14

Martial arts · 16

A day out · 18

Going to the theater · 20

Music · 22

Dance · 24

Exhibitions · 26

Stories and reading · 28

Glossary · 30

Index · 32

Contenido

La diversión por todo el mundo · 4

Juegos de mesa y cartas · 6

Juegos de niños · 8

Carreras y competencias · 10

Los Juegos Olímpicos · 12

El fútbol · 14

Las artes marciales · 16

De excursión · 18

Vamos al teatro · 20

La música · 22

El baile · 24

Las exposiciones · 26

Historias y lectura · 28

Glosario · 30

Índice · 32

To read this book in English, follow the orange boxes. To read this book in Spanish, follow the blue boxes. Look for the globe on each page. It shows you where each country is in the world and on which continent.

Para leer este libro en inglés, sigue los recuadros en anaranjado. Para leer este libro en español, sigue los recuadros en azul. Busca el globo terráqueo en cada página. Te muestra dónde está ubicado cada país en el mundo y en qué continente.

Fun around the world

La diversión por todo el mundo

All over the world, there are a lot of ways to have fun. Let's visit some countries to compare different games and other entertainment.

En todo el mundo hay muchas maneras de divertirse. Vamos a visitar algunos países para comparar diferentes juegos y otras formas de ocio.

MOZAMBIQUE

Games can be made out of anything! In Mozambique, a *galimoto* is a toy made from bits of wood and wire and pushed along with a stick.

MOZAMBIQUE

¡Los juegos pueden hacerse con cualquier cosa! En Mozambique, un galimoto es un juguete hecho de trozos de madera y alambre y empujado con un palo.

4

UKRAINE

Performances by dancers is one form of entertainment. In Ukraine, people love to go to the ballet to see great dancers perform.

UCRANIA

Las actuaciones de danza son una forma de ocio. En Ucrania, a la gente le encanta ir al *ballet* para ver actuar a grandes bailarines.

MOZAMBIQUE
MOZAMBIQUE

UKRAINE
UCRANIA

Asia/Asia

Europe/
Europa

África/
África

Australia/
Oceanía

What is entertainment?

Entertainment is something you enjoy. It can be anything you do, look at, or listen to—and it's fun!

¿Qué es el ocio?

El ocio es algo que disfrutas. Puede ser cualquier cosa que hagas, mires o escuches, ¡y que sea sea divertida!

Board games and cards

People of all ages enjoy board games and card games. Some board games involve great skill and lots of practice.

MADAGASCAR

Fanorona is a board game that comes from Madagascar. To win, you have to capture the other player's pieces.

Juegos de mesa y cartas

La gente de todas las edades disfruta con los juegos de mesa y los juegos de cartas. Algunos juegos de mesa requieren gran habilidad y mucha práctica.

MADAGASCAR

La Fanorona es un juego de mesa de Madagascar. Para ganar tienes que capturar las fichas del otro jugador.

RUSSIA

Russians are famous for playing chess. It can take years of practice to get good at the game! Children join chess clubs while they are still at school.

RUSIA

Los rusos son famosos por jugar al ajedrez. ¡Puede llevar años de práctica llegar a jugar bien! Los niños se unen a clubs de ajedrez cuando aún están en la escuela.

MADAGASCAR
MADAGASCAR

RUSSIA
RUSIA

Asia/Asia

Europe/
Europa

Africa/
África

Australia/
Oceanía

Playing cards

Around the world, card games, such as crazy eights, are very popular. The games change from country to country.

Jugar a las cartas

Por todo el mundo, los juegos de cartas, como el *ocho loco*, son muy populares. Los juegos varían de un país a otro.

7

Children's games

Most children love to play games outdoors. They often chase each other or hide from one another! Around the world, they play different **versions** of the same games.

CUBA

In Cuba, children play a version of the game redlight, greenlight, or statues. If you are seen moving when you are supposed to be frozen, you are out!

Juegos de niños

A la mayoría de los niños les encanta jugar al aire libre. ¡A menudo se persiguen unos a otros o se esconden unos de otros! Por todo el mundo juegan **versiones** diferentes de los mismos juegos.

CUBA

En Cuba, los niños juegan a una versión del juego del un, dos, tres, toca la pared o juego de las estatuas. ¡Si ven que te mueves cuando se supone que deberías estar quieto estás fuera!

SOUTH AFRICA

Hopscotch in South Africa is a popular game. Children draw squares on the ground and hop from one square to the other.

SUDÁFRICA

La rayuela es un juego popular en Sudáfrica. Para jugar, los niños dibujan cuadrados en el suelo y luego saltan de un cuadrado al otro.

North America/ América del Norte

Europe/ Europa

Africa/ África

South America/ América del Sur

CUBA

CUBA

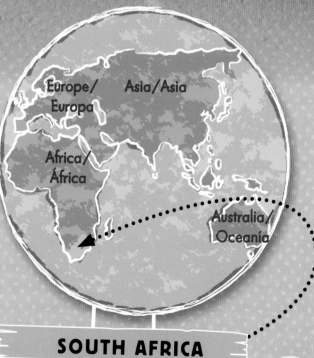

Europe/ Europa

Asia/Asia

Africa/ África

Australia/ Oceanía

SOUTH AFRICA

SUDÁFRICA

9

Races and competitions

Many games are also **competitions**. People in all countries enjoy watching competitions, especially races.

AUSTRALIA

For recreation, sailing is a popular activity in Australia. Many sailors like to take part in races. People watch the races from motorboats or along the shore.

Carreras y competencias

Muchos juegos son también **competencias**. En todos los países la gente disfruta viendo competencias, sobre todo carreras.

AUSTRALIA

Navegar a vela es una popular actividad recreativa en Australia. A muchos navegantes les gusta participar en carreras. La gente ve las carreras desde lanchas motoras o desde la orilla.

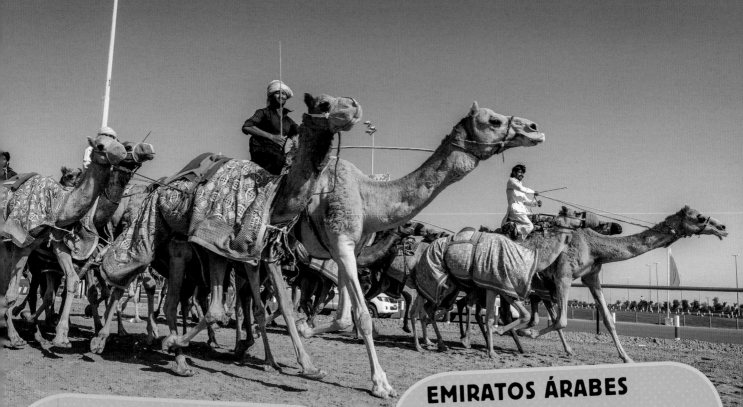

UNITED ARAB EMIRATES

Camels are an important animal in United Arab Emirates. Camel racing is a tradition. People love watching the camels and riders race around the track as fast as they can!

EMIRATOS ÁRABES UNIDOS

Los camellos son un animal importante en los Emiratos Árabes Unidos. Montar en camello en tradicionales. ¡A la gente le encanta ver a los camellos y jinetes compitiendo por la pista tan rápido como pueden!

What is recreation?

Recreation is an activity that is not work. It includes things you do for fun and in your spare time, such as sports and other hobbies.

¿Qué es una actividad recreativa?

Una actividad recreativa es una actividad que no es trabajo. Incluye las cosas que haces por diversión en tu tiempo libre, como el deporte y otras aficiones.

UNITED ARAB EMIRATES
EMIRATOS ÁRABES UNIDOS

Europe/ Europa

Asia/Asia

África/ África

Australia/ Oceanía

AUSTRALIA
AUSTRALIA

11

Olympic Games

The biggest competitions in the world are the Olympic Games. Most countries send teams to compete. There are summer games and winter games.

POLAND

Volleyball is one of Poland's most popular sports. Polish people watch and cheer for their **national** team in the summer Olympics.

Los Juegos Olímpicos

Las mayores competencias del mundo son los Juegos Olímpicos. La mayoría de las naciones envían equipos a competir. Hay juegos de verano y juegos de invierno.

POLONIA

El vóleibol es uno de los deportes más populares de Polonia. Los polacos miran y animan a su equipo **nacional** en los Juegos Olímpicos de verano.

FINLAND

Finland has a lot of snow and many snowboarding champions. People love to see them jump during the winter Olympics.

FINLANDIA

Finlandia tiene mucha nieve y muchos campeones del *snowboard*. A la gente le encanta verlos saltar durante las Olimpíadas de invierno.

FINLAND

FINLANDIA

Europe/
Europa

Asia/Asia

África/
África

Australia/
Oceanía

POLAND

POLONIA

The Olympics

The Olympics take place every four years. The games move to different countries each time.

Los Juegos Olímpicos

Los Juegos Olímpicos tienen lugar cada cuatro años. Los juegos se trasladan a diferentes países cada vez.

Football and soccer

El fútbol

Football is the most popular game in the world. But the name football means different games in different parts of the world.

El fútbol es el juego más popular del mundo, pero el nombre fútbol se refiere a distintos juegos en diferentes partes del mundo.

MOROCCO

In many parts of the world, football means the game of soccer. It is Morocco's favorite sport. Children can play it in any open space.

MARRUECOS

En muchas partes del mundo, el fútbol se refiere al juego de patear la pelota. Es el deporte favorito de Marruecos. Los niños lo pueden jugar en cualquier lugar donde haya un espacio abierto.

What is your favorite sport?

¿Cuál es tu deporte favorito?

14

UNITED STATES
ESTADOS UNIDOS

North America/
América del Norte

Europe/
Europa

África/
África

South America/
América del Sur

MOROCCO
MARRUECOS

UNITED STATES

In the United States, football and soccer are different games. Football is a game in which players throw the ball and run with it. The other team tries to get it.

ESTADOS UNIDOS

En los Estados Unidos, el fútbol americano y el fútbol son juegos diferentes. En el fútbol americano los jugadores lanzan la pelota y corren con ella mientras el otro equipo intenta atraparla.

Martial arts

Las artes marciales

The martial arts started as a way of fighting that could be used for **self-defense**. Now martial arts are practiced as sports for fitness, fun, and competition.

Las artes marciales comenzaron como una forma de lucha que podía ser usada para la **autodefensa**. Ahora las artes marciales se practican para estar en forma, como diversión y en competencias.

NORTH KOREA

Many traditional martial arts come from Asian countries. Taekwondo began in Korea. Children learn Taekwondo at classes after school.

COREA DEL NORTE

Muchas artes marciales tradicionales vienen de los países asiáticos. El taekwondo comenzó en Corea. Los niños aprenden taekwondo en clases después de la escuela.

Europe/
Europa

Asia/Asia

Africa/
África

Australia/
Oceanía

NORTH KOREA

COREA DEL NORTE

BRAZIL

The martial art capoeira is part of Brazil's heritage. It is a mix of martial arts, dance, and acrobatics. Capoeira shows usually have music and singing, too.

BRASIL

La capoeira es un arte marcial que forma parte del patrimonio de Brasil. Es una mezcla de artes marciales, baile y acrobacia. Los espectáculos de capoeira normalmente también tienen música y canciones.

BRAZIL

BRASIL

Europe/
Europa

North
America/
América
del Norte

África/
África

South
America/
América
del Sur

17

A day out

There are many kinds of entertainment in the world. Entertainment can include exciting trips, such as going to the zoo or to see a show.

CANADA

The Cirque du Soleil circus started in Canada and is famous around the world. The shows include amazing acrobatics and dazzling light shows.

De excursión

Hay muchos tipos de ocio en el mundo. El ocio incluye excursiones emocionantes, como ir al zoológico o ver un espectáculo.

CANADÁ

El circo Cirque du Soleil comenzó en Canadá y es famoso en todo el mundo. Las actuaciones incluyen acrobacias increíbles y espectáculos de luces deslumbrantes.

SPAIN

Zoos are places where people can see wild animals up close. In Spain, animals at the Bioparc in Valencia live in landscapes just like their natural **habitats**.

ESPAÑA

Los zoológicos son lugares donde la gente puede ver animales salvajes de cerca. En España, los animales del Bioparc de Valencia viven en entornos iguales a su **hábitat** natural.

Popular trips

Other popular trips include going to the beach, the park, the movies, museums, and historical sites.

Excursiones populares

Otras excursiones populares incluyen ir a la playa, al parque, al cine, a museos y a sitios históricos.

CANADA
CANADÁ

North America/ América del Norte

Europe/ Europa

Africa/ África

South America/ América del Sur

SPAIN
ESPAÑA

19

Going to the theater

Vamos al teatro

Theater began as ceremonies performed long ago. Today, theater usually means a play with actors. Many countries have traditional kinds of theater.

El teatro comenzó con rituales representados hace mucho tiempo. Hoy, el teatro normalmente es una obra con actores. Muchos países tienen teatro detipo tradicional.

JAPAN

Plays called Kabuki often show events in Japan's history. The actors paint their faces and wear traditional costumes.

JAPÓN

Las obras de teatro llamadas Kabuki a menudo muestran acontecimientos de la historia. Los actores se pintan la cara y visten trajes tradicionales.

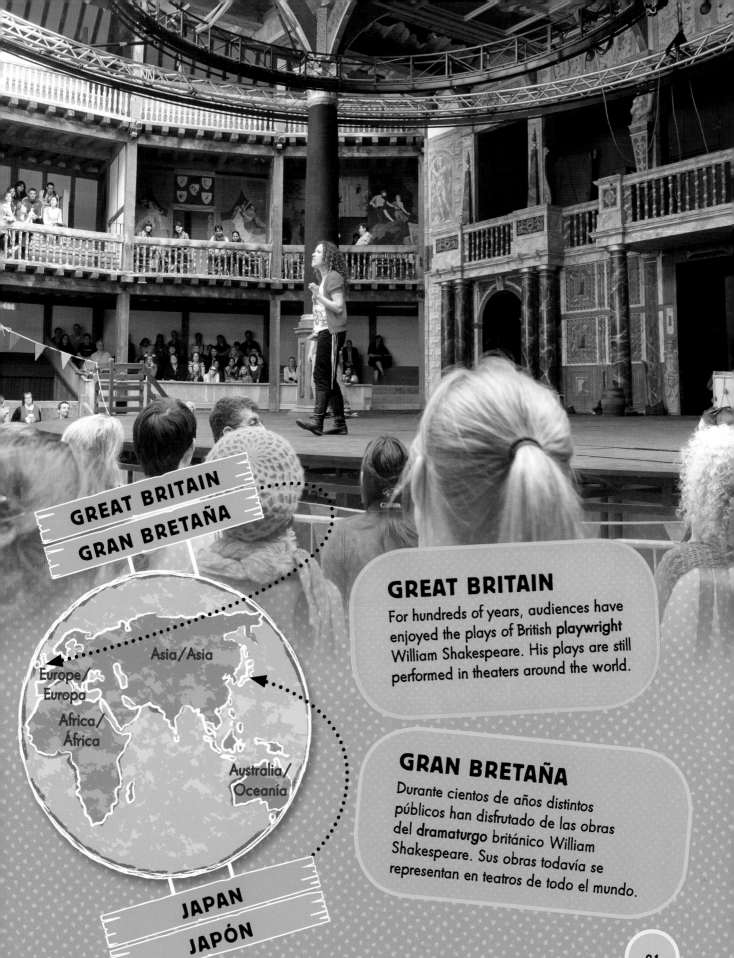

GREAT BRITAIN
GRAN BRETAÑA

Asia/Asia

Europe/
Europa

África/
África

Australia/
Oceanía

JAPAN
JAPÓN

GREAT BRITAIN

For hundreds of years, audiences have enjoyed the plays of British **playwright** William Shakespeare. His plays are still performed in theaters around the world.

GRAN BRETAÑA

Durante cientos de años distintos públicos han disfrutado de las obras del **dramaturgo** británico William Shakespeare. Sus obras todavía se representan en teatros de todo el mundo.

Music

Most people like listening to music! Some music is played for special occasions, such as **parades**. Other music is part of everyday life.

IRELAND

Towns in Ireland celebrate St. Patrick's Day with music, dancing, and parades. People love to listen to brass bands as they march by in the parade.

La música

¡A la mayoría de la gente le gusta escuchar música! Cierta música se toca en ocasiones especiales, como los **desfiles**. Otra música forma parte de la vida diaria.

IRLANDA

Los pueblos de Irlanda celebran el Día de San Patricio con música, baile y desfiles. A la gente le encanta escuchar las bandas de música cuando marchan en el desfile.

IRELAND
IRLANDA

INDIA

Musicians in India perform in the street for everyone to enjoy. They sing and play traditional instruments.

INDIA

Los músicos de la India actúan en la calle para que todo el mundo disfrute. Cantan y tocan instrumentos tradicionales.

Europe/
Europa

Asia/Asia

África/
África

Australia/
Oceanía

INDIA
INDIA

What kinds of music do you like?

¿Qué tipos de música te gustan?

Dance

El baile

Where there is music, there is often dancing. People everywhere like to dance, and dancing is fun to watch, too!

Donde hay música, a menudo hay baile. En todas partes a la gente le gusta bailar, ¡y ver bailar es divertido también!

NEW ZEALAND

The Maori people of New Zealand do a traditional dance using a ball called a *poi*. They sing, dance, and swing the *poi* in patterns.

NUEVA ZELANDA

Los maoríes de Nueva Zelanda hacen un baile tradicional usando una pelota llamada *poi*. Cantan, bailan y mueven el *poi* haciendo figuras.

PHILIPPINES

Tinikling is a traditional dance in the Philippines. People move poles back and forth and together in a rhythm. Dancers have to jump in and out between the moving poles.

Asia/Asia

North América/ América del Norte

South America/ América del Sur

Australia/ Oceanía

FILIPINAS

El Tinikling es un baile tradicional de las Filipinas. La gente mueve varas de bambú de un lado a otro en conjunto siguiendo un ritmo. Los bailarines tienen que saltar dentro y fuera entre las varas que se mueven.

NEW ZEALAND

NUEVA ZELANDA

Exhibitions

Las exposiciones

An **exhibition** can be a show of art, such as paintings or sculpture. Museums also have exhibitions where you can learn about science, history, or nature.

Una **exposición** puede ser una muestra de arte, como cuadros o escultura. Los museos también tienen exposiciones donde puedes aprender sobre la ciencia, la historia o la naturaleza.

FRANCE

The Louvre is a huge museum in Paris. People travel there from all over the world to see famous works of art.

FRANCIA

El Louvre es un enorme museo de París. La gente viaja allí desde todo el mundo para ver famosas obras de arte.

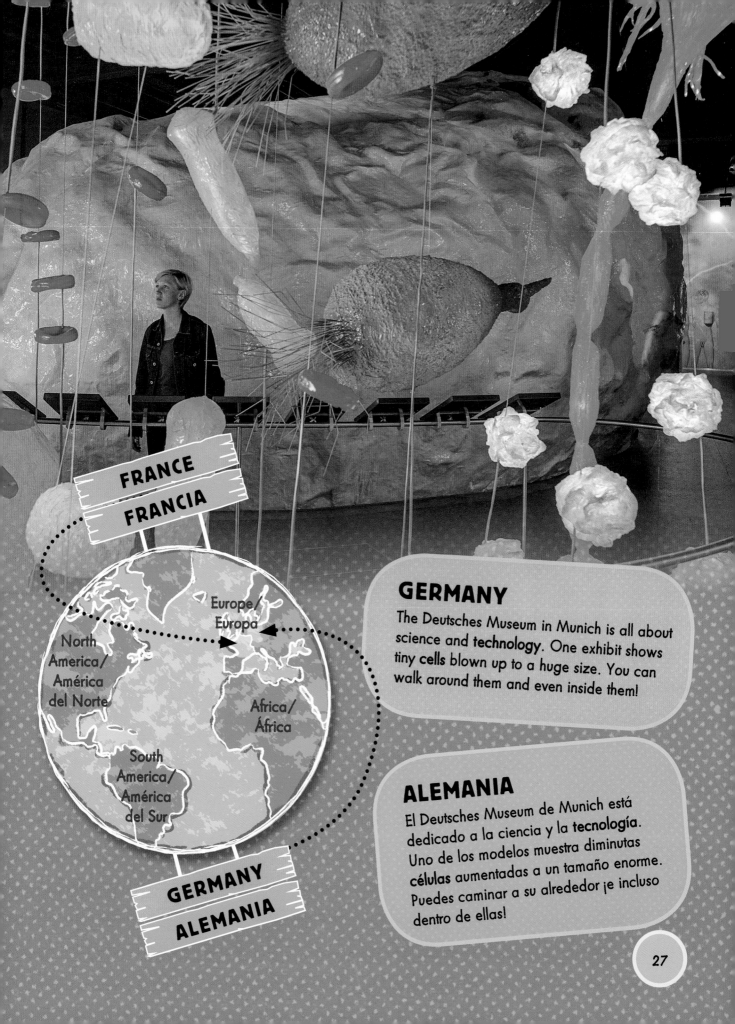

FRANCE
FRANCIA

North
America/
América
del Norte

Europe/
Europa

Africa/
África

South
America/
América
del Sur

GERMANY
ALEMANIA

GERMANY

The Deutsches Museum in Munich is all about
science and technology. One exhibit shows
tiny cells blown up to a huge size. You can
walk around them and even inside them!

ALEMANIA

El Deutsches Museum de Munich está
dedicado a la ciencia y la tecnología.
Uno de los modelos muestra diminutas
células aumentadas a un tamaño enorme.
Puedes caminar a su alrededor ¡e incluso
dentro de ellas!

27

Stories and reading

Countries around the world have their own myths, legends, and other stories. The stories entertain people and keep a traditional **culture** alive.

PAKISTAN

In Pakistan, older people are often the storytellers in a **community**. They pass on stories to children and grandchildren.

Historias y lectura

Por todo el mundo los países tienen sus propios mitos, leyendas y otras historias. Las historias entretienen a la gente y mantienen viva la **cultura** tradicional.

PAKISTÁN

En Pakistán, las personas mayores son a menudo los narradores de la **comunidad**. Pasan las historias a hijos y nietos.

CHINA

CHINA

Asia/Asia

Europe/
Europa

Africa/
África

Australia/
Oceanía

PAKISTAN

PAKISTÁN

What are myths and legends?

Legends and myths are stories passed down through time. Legends may include real heroes and events. Myths often tell tales of magical or imaginary characters.

¿Qué son mitos y leyendas?

Las leyendas y los mitos son historias transmitidas a través del tiempo. Las leyendas pueden incluir héroes y sucesos reales. Los mitos a menudo cuentan relatos de personajes mágicos o imaginarios.

CHINA

Families in China often spend hours in bookstores reading books. If you have a book, you can always entertain yourself!

CHINA

En China, las familias a menudo pasan horas en las librerías leyendo libros. ¡Si tienes un libro, siempre puedes entretenerte!

29

Glossary

acrobatics Performance of difficult and amazing acts, such as balancing and jumping

cell One of the parts that all living things are made of. Cells have many shapes and are usually too small to see without a microscope.

ceremonies Events that use traditional actions, objects, and words

community A group of people that live near each other, such as people in a tribe, village, or neighborhood

competition A game or sporting event where one team or person wins over others

culture A combination of beliefs and customs that belong to a particular group of people

exhibition A display in a public place, such as a museum

habitat The place where a living thing belongs and lives

heritage Anything that is passed down to you from your family or culture

imaginary Not real

national Having to do with a nation. A national team is the team that represents a particular nation.

parade A moving line or crowd of people, often joined by marching bands. Parades happen at carnivals, festivals, and important occasions.

playwright The author of a play

popular Liked by a lot of people

recreation Activities that are not work and that are done for fun

rhythm A regular pattern of sound or movement, such as the beat of music

self-defense Protecting yourself

skill An ability to do something very well, especially something learned with practice or training

technology Scientific knowledge, processes, or tools that people can use to do things, for example, the use of computers for work or learning

traditional Always done in the same way and passed on to younger people in a family or community

version Something, such as a game, that is done a bit differently to other ways of doing it. Stories often have different versions, too.

Glosario

(acrobatics) acrobacia Presentación de actos difíciles y sorprendentes, como equilibrio o saltos

(cell) célula Una de las partes de las que están hechos todos los seres vivos. Las células tienen muchas formas y normalmente son demasiado pequeñas para verlas sin un microscopio.

(ceremonies) ceremonias Eventos que incluyen acciones, objetos y palabras tradicionales

(community) comunidad Grupo de personas que viven cerca unos de otros, como las personas de una tribu, un pueblo o un barrio

(competition) competencia Juego o evento deportivo en el que un equipo o una persona gana a los otros

(culture) cultura Combinación de creencias y costumbres que pertenecen a un grupo de personas en particular

(exhibition) exposición Presentación en un lugar público, como un museo

(habitat) hábitat El lugar al que pertenece y donde vive un ser viviente

(heritage) patrimonio Cualquier cosa que te transmite tu familia o cultura

(imaginary) imaginario No real

(national) nacional Que tiene que ver con una nación. Un equipo nacional es el equipo que representa a una nación en particular.

(parade) desfile Fila de personas o multitud en movimiento, a menudo acompañadas por bandas de música. Los desfiles tienen lugar en carnavales, festivales y ocasiones importantes.

(playwright) dramaturgo El autor de una obra de teatro

(popular) popular Que gusta a mucha gente

(recreation) actividad recreativa Actividad que no es trabajo y que se hace por diversión

(rhythm) ritmo Patrón regular de sonido o movimiento, como el compás de la música

(self-defense) autodefensa Protegerte a ti mismo

(skill) habilidad La capacidad de hacer algo muy bien, sobre todo algo aprendido con la práctica o el entrenamiento

(technology) tecnología Conocimiento, procesos o instrumentos científicos que se pueden usar para hacer cosas, por ejemplo, usar computadoras para trabajar o aprender

(traditional) tradicional Hecho siempre de la misma manera y pasado a los miembros más jóvenes de una familia o comunidad

(version) versión Algo, por ejemplo un juego, que se hace de manera un poco diferente a otras maneras de hacerlo. Las historias a menudo tienen también diferentes versiones.

Index

Índice

acrobatics 17, 18
Australia 10, 11
ballet 5
board games 6, 7
books 29
Brazil 17
camel races 11
Canada 18, 19
capoeira 17
card games 6, 7
chess 7
children's games 8, 9
China 29
circus 18
competitions 10, 11, 12, 13, 16
Cuba 8, 9
dancing 5, 17, 22, 24, 25
exhibitions 26, 27
Fanorona 6
Finland 13
football 14, 15
France 26, 27
fun 4, 5, 11, 16, 24
Germany 27
Great Britain 21
India 23
Ireland 22, 23
Japan 20, 21
Kabuki plays 20
legends 28, 29
Madagascar 6, 7
Maori 24
marching bands 22
martial arts 16, 17
Morocco 14, 15
Mozambique 4, 5
museums 19, 26, 27

music 17, 22, 23, 24
myths 28, 29
New Zealand 24, 25
North Korea 16, 17
Olympic Games 12, 13
Pakistan 28, 29
parades 22
performances 5, 17, 18, 20, 21, 24, 25
Philippines 25
Poland 12, 13
races 10, 11
reading 29
recreation 10, 11
Russia 7
sailing 10
St. Patrick's Day 22
Shakespeare, William 21
snowboarding 13
soccer 14, 15
South Africa 9
Spain 19
sports 11, 12, 13, 14, 15
storytelling 28
taekwondo 16
teams 12, 14, 15
theater 20, 21
Tinikling 25
toys 4
trips 18, 19
Ukraine 5
United Arab Emirates 11
United States 15
volleyball 12
zoo 18, 19

acrobacia 17, 18
actividad recreativa 10, 11
actuaciones 5, 17, 18, 20, 21, 24, 25
ajedrez 7
Alemania 27
artes marciales 16, 17
Australia 10, 11
baile 5, 17, 22, 24, 25
ballet 5
bandas de música 22
Brasil 17
Canadá 18, 19
Capoeira 17
carreras 10, 11
carreras de camellos 11
China 29
circo 18
competencias 10, 11, 12, 13, 16
Corea del Norte 16, 17
Cuba 8, 9
deporte 11, 12, 13, 14, 15
desfiles 22
Día de San Patricio 22
diversión 4, 5, 11, 16, 24
Emiratos Árables Unidos 11
equipos 12, 14, 15
España 19
Estados Unidos 15
excursiones 18, 19
exposiciones 26, 27
Fanorona 6
Filipinas 25
Finlandia 13

Francia 26, 27
fútbol 14, 15
fútbol americano 15
Gran Bretaña 21
historias 28
India 23
Irlanda 22, 23
Japón 20, 21
juegos de cartas 6, 7
juegos de mesa 6, 7
juegos de niños 8, 9
Juegos Olímpicos 12, 13
juguetes 4
lectura 29
leyendas 28, 29
libros 29
Madagascar 6, 7
maorí 24
Marruecos 14, 15
mitos 28, 29
Mozambique 4, 5
museos 19, 26, 27
música 17, 22, 23, 24
navegación 10
Nueva Zelanda 24, 25
Pakistán 28, 29
Polonia 12, 13
Rusia 7
Shakespeare, William 21
snowboard 13
Sudáfrica 9
taekwondo 16
teatro 20, 21
teatro Kabuki 20
Tinikling 25
Ucrania 5
vóleibol 12
zoo 18, 19

El índice español no sigue el mismo orden que el inglés.